Widow Inheritance and Contested Citizenship in Kenya

This book examines the practice of widow inheritance in order to explore the intersection between power, gender and sexualities in Kenya.

Using widow inheritance amongst the Luo of Kenya as a case study, the book explores the role of body politics in the construction of gendered subjects and nations. *Widow Inheritance and Contested Citizenship in Kenya* unpacks how 'respectable femininities' and 'wayward sexualities' become the 'sites' within which national and state politics are ritualized and where tensions resulting from non-hegemonic performances of both gender and sexuality are 'resolved'. The empirical research that underpins this book is qualitative and grounded in feminist methodology, challenging the erasure of women's narratives in hegemonic epistemologies.

Widow Inheritance and Contested Citizenship in Kenya will be of interest to students and scholars of African gender studies and women's rights.

Awino Okech is a lecturer at the Centre for Gender Studies, School of Oriental and African Studies, London and a Senior Research Associate with the African Leadership Centre, Kings College London.

Routledge Studies on Gender and Sexuality in Africa

The Tunisian Women's Rights Movement
From Nascent Activism to Influential Power-broking
Jane D. Tchaicha and Khédija Arfaoui

Disability and Sexuality in Zimbabwe
Voices from the Periphery
Christine Peta

Love, Sex and Teenage Sexual Cultures in South Africa
16 Turning 17
Deevia Bhana

African Women, ICT and Neoliberal Politics
The Challenge of Gendered Digital Divides to People-Centered Governance
Assata Zerai

Widow Inheritance and Contested Citizenship in Kenya
Awino Okech

Widow Inheritance and Contested Citizenship in Kenya

Awino Okech

LONDON AND NEW YORK

First published 2019
by Routledge
2 Park Square, Milton Park, Abingdon, Oxon OX14 4RN

and by Routledge
52 Vanderbilt Avenue, New York, NY 10017

Routledge is an imprint of the Taylor & Francis Group, an informa business

© 2019 Awino Okech

The right of Awino Okech to be identified as author of this work has been asserted by her in accordance with sections 77 and 78 of the Copyright, Designs and Patents Act 1988.

All rights reserved. No part of this book may be reprinted or reproduced or utilised in any form or by any electronic, mechanical, or other means, now known or hereafter invented, including photocopying and recording, or in any information storage or retrieval system, without permission in writing from the publishers.

Trademark notice: Product or corporate names may be trademarks or registered trademarks, and are used only for identification and explanation without intent to infringe.

British Library Cataloguing-in-Publication Data
A catalogue record for this book is available from the British Library

Library of Congress Cataloging-in-Publication Data
A catalog record for this book has been requested

ISBN: 978-0-367-07767-9 (hbk)
ISBN: 978-0-429-02271-5 (ebk)

Typeset in Times New Roman
by Apex CoVantage, LLC

For Mama

Contents

Acknowledgements ix

Introduction 1
Methodology 2
Research methods 4
Memory and truth 5
Structure 6

1 Gender, sexuality and culture 10
'African culture' and gender 11
Gender post flag independence 12
Body politics and sexuality 15
Continuities: debates on sexuality in Kenya 17

2 Dominant discourses on widow inheritance 20
Widow inheritance as a 'cultural practice' 20
Ties that bind: heterosexual marital bonds 21
Becoming a Luo widow 23
Widow inheritance: disembodied and disciplining ritual practices 26
HIV/AIDS: disease as a vector 28
Religion as a trope 32
Women's rights and widow inheritance 34
Conclusion 37

3 Widow inheritance and gender identity 41
Politics of gender 42
Wayward femininities 49
Respectable femininities and reproduction 53
Conclusion 55

4 Discursive boundaries: building nations 57
Constructing boundaries and defining borders 57
The 'insider' 58
The 'outsider' – Jamwa *59*
Conclusion 64

5 Gendered language and culture 66
Gendered linguistic practices 67
Metaphors, silences and subversion 72
Conclusion 73

6 Conclusion 75

Bibliography 79
Index 90

Acknowledgements

The research that informs this book was made possible by the Steve Biko Leadership Fellowship between 2008–2009.

I would like to thank the research participants whose discussions generated the data for and in this dissertation, the women and men who entertained my 'prying' questions and opened their homes to me; this book is a product of your reflections.

I am indebted to my supervisor Professor Jane Bennett who supported the development of this work when I was a PhD researcher.

To Funmi Olonisakin for working with me through many writing blocks. To my family for their support during my PhD journey.

Finally, to and for my mother Dolphine Achieng, who sparked my interest in this topic. Even though you are no longer here, I hope that this research contributes in some measure to the work you began.

Introduction

I am neither a widow, nor from a developing country. My husband has not recently died from AIDS, nor do I face the prospect of being inherited by one of my husband's relatives, typically a brother. What property I do own will not be grabbed or seized by my husband's family after his death, leaving me and my children, if they are not taken away from me, destitute. I will not be forced to have sex with one of my husband's relatives to cleanse me. I will not be blamed for my husband's death, accused of witchcraft or ostracised from my family or community as a result of the stigma attached to AIDS. With no male to depend on, it won't be necessary for me to resort to activities that are considered immoral by the society in which I live, such as commercial sex work or beer brewing and selling, and which could place me and others at risk of further infection
(Sleap, 2001: 2)

The excerpt above exemplifies dominant analysis on widow inheritance. Underlying these narratives is the construction of African women's sexualities and bodies around discourses on disease, harmful traditional practices or violence. In sum, even though they are desirous of freedom they are shaped by constraint. These generalisations while informed by the intention to seek women's rights including those associated with bodily autonomy and therefore sexual pleasure, often wish away the many ways in which women and gender specifically is negotiated across different contexts. Literature and activism on widow inheritance across Africa has often followed a pattern identified by McFadden (2003) with an emphasis of the lack of agency of women and thereby positioning 'cultural practices' as only capable of being read within binaries: modernity/ urbanity/Christianity and tradition/rurality/ civilisation.

This book contributes to a body of African feminist scholarship that takes seriously the intersection between power, gender and sexualities (see Bennett, 2003; Lewis, 2003, 2004; McFadden, 2003; Mupotsa & Mhishi, 2008;

Pereira, 2005; Tamale, 2005). Sexuality serves as the analytical frame to examine how femininity – and therefore masculinity – become mobilised within broad and volatile debates on rights, power and national identity in Kenya. I explore the role of body politics in the construction of gendered subjects and nations through an analysis of discourses on widow inheritance amongst the Luo of Kenya. The inherent tension manifested in the preservation of 'cultural norms' – the framework within which the surveillance of women's sexuality occurs – and ethnic identities becomes apparent. The discourses that emerge around the performance of 'good womanhood' point to the nexus between power and pleasure as key to the emergence of 'respectable femininities' and 'wayward sexualities', as routes used by women to subvert the control of their sexual and bodily autonomy. Consequently, debates about women's sexuality in general, reproduction and communities' physical and metaphorical borders come into sharp focus. 'Respectable femininities' and 'wayward sexualities' become the 'sites' from which national and state politics are ritualised and where tensions resulting from non-hegemonic performances of both gender and sexuality are 'resolved'.

The analysis drawn from my empirical research points to the fact that normative descriptions of femininity and masculinity are contested and subverted within expected widow inheritance rites. Women who have been predominantly construed as oppressed find ways to work within the cultural constraints imposed upon them to secure the right to housing, ownership of property and sexual agency – read here as the right to choose a sexual partner or not, the choice to have children and the choice to not be de-sexualised because they refuse to acquiesce to cultural norms. Power relations are constantly negotiated, shifting and changing through everyday acts of bodily resistance. The analysis in this book is not intended to offer a collective description of widow inheritance. Instead, I explore how descriptions of diverse experiences of widow inheritance give rise to discourses on gender, sexuality, power and identity. It is the discourses produced during the narration of experiences rather than the experiences themselves that my research analysed.

Methodology

The empirical research that underpins this book is qualitative and grounded in feminist methodology. This means that both the theoretical framework and research methods paid attention to 'what is not asked', thereby contributing to transforming what constitutes knowledge and how knowledge 'production' is understood (Bennett, 2008; Foucault, 1978). I draw on a theoretical tradition that views gender as constructed and performative even though the daily negotiations of gender during my field work functioned within paradigms that took patriarchy as given (Butler, 1990; Pereira, 2005; Rubin, 1984; Stoler, 2002). Heterosexuality is therefore foregrounded as one of the ways in which patriarchy and therefore gender and sexuality are reinforced in daily practices and norms by legitimising some performances of gender and sexuality as correct and others as incorrect. Critically examining institutions such as the family, the clan, the state and the market as routes through which sexual and political ordering occurs is therefore key (Douglas, 2002; McClintock, 1995; Stoler, 2002; Thomas, 2005; Yuval-Davis & Anthias, 1989).

My research was conducted in sections of Kisumu East District, specifically in Kadibo division in the villages of Kadibo, K'akoko and K'ayim. This is an area that is best described as peri-urban, given its proximity to Kisumu, the third largest city in Kenya. Participant selection was shaped by a review of literature, which led to mapping key interlocutors for my study. The seemingly homogeneous categories described below did not limit my engagement with participants solely within these boundaries, but rather conversations often involved a mix of individuals. At other times, I worked within the categories described below. I adopted purposive sampling, which means that I targeted people who possessed the attributes or histories being studied. I also utilised snowball sampling, where participants referred me to other individuals who had similar narratives or were central to their own stories. The participants were identified through a community organiser I had previously worked with on development initiatives in the region.

The first set of participants were widows between the ages of 25–50 years old. I wanted to ensure that I was working with women whose husbands had died within the last ten years, which was the period of focus for my study. This broad age group, although useful for setting initial parameters, did not hold during the actual field work, since some of the older matriarchs within the homes where the focus group discussions (FGDs) were held became participants. Other variables, such as the type of marriage (monogamous or polygamous) and the cause of spousal death, were not specified as factors that would influence the sampling process. This omission was intentional since the broad objectives of my research were not driven by generating data that would distinguish between categories of women that have already been largely pathologised as vulnerable and oppressed within dominant literature of widow inheritance. This choice enabled an organic engagement with these factors when they emerged as part of the interviews and FGDs. All the women considered themselves Christians and had completed secondary school education.

The second group of research participants were levirates (*joter*) and 'ritual cleansers' (*jokowiny*). I distinguish between levirates and ritual cleansers, who are often conflated in most literature on widow inheritance in Kenya.[1] However, most of the men who were interviewed simply defined themselves as levirates even though triangulation revealed the contrary. This decision was due to local constructions of ritual cleansers as businessmen who have commercialised the practice. Although *joter* and *jokowiny* were key groups, it was difficult to find a significant number of men who were willing to speak about their experiences; hence, there were fewer interviewed than the widows. The final group of research participants were key informants:

4 *Introduction*

cultural custodians, including representatives of the Luo Council of Elders, chiefs and local clan elders. I initially referred to this category of participants as key informants; individuals who could be defined as knowledgeable resource persons and were gatekeepers who, if left out of the process or not consulted, could have a negative impact on my work. When I began my work, some of the 'holders of knowledge' turned out to be patriarchs and matriarchs in some homesteads, teachers or clan elders.

Research methods

Focus group discussions (FGDs) and key informant interviews were the key methods for data generation from 60 research participants, whom I worked with over one year. I conducted 30 interviews; six were with individuals identified as 'inheritors', three were with key informants, 11 were with widows and ten were triangulations with in-laws and other relations of the widows and 'inheritors'. In addition, six FGDs were conducted over a period of four months with 60 women and men. All FGDs consisted of women and men across different age brackets. Two main analytical approaches shaped how I worked with the material from the FGDs: discourse and conversation analysis. FGDs elicit a variety of linguistic genres, such as questions, explanations and narratives in the form of anecdotes. Analytically, discourse and conversation analysis were the main ways I worked with the material from the FGDs. This meant that in some instances I deployed a form of conversation analysis, where emphasis was placed on the positioning of speakers (the sites from which the speaker derives their authority) and how this informed the construction and production of specific subjectivities. It also meant paying attention to the ways in which gender and power were negotiated and space organised and/or arrogated. In using discourse analysis, I collected content across FGDs to develop discourse, followed by an analysis of discursive devices, as they presented themselves during the FGD conversations.

In using these analytical methods, I was cognisant of two key methodological insights. The first was the context of the research, which was shaped by a political crisis that had been triggered by a contested presidential election in 2007. The ability to separate the data generated during this period from the political moment is at best tenuous. The political debates in Kenya, in the aftermath of the post-election crisis in Kenya in 2008, had implications for gendered bodies and citizenship. These debates discursively recast the function of widow inheritance as shall be discussed later in this book. These events had implications for gendered bodies and citizenship, and discursively re-cast the function of widow inheritance. The second methodological insight concerns the practicalities of working across two different languages (Dho'Luo and English) and the complexities of using discourse analysis in a context where I sought not to represent the narratives through a process of translation but rather to represent them whilst being alert to their 'un-translatability'.

Memory and truth

My research as noted previously drew, in part, on the interpretation of narratives emerging from the FGDs as a means of interrogating larger systemic discourses of gender, sexuality, the nation and state. Although the focus groups involved more than narratives exchanged between participants themselves, and with me, the narrative content of the focus group conversations forms key elements of the data under analysis in Chapters 3, 4 and 5. Narratives are often constructed as life histories and are derivative of first-person accounts of social phenomena, thus relying on the interpretation of events. This leads to questions about the validity of such data (i.e. how empirical is it?). The validity and empiricism question responds to the challenge of overreliance on the memory of the narrator and the possibility of many truths. Do narratives, for instance, offer a substantive basis for making a persuasive argument that allows a researcher to understand the social phenomena that it sets up? Does the micro level – the individual life stories or cumulative narratives collected via interviews, FGDs or participant observation – allow us to understand the macro level – i.e. the larger social concerns that we are interested in understanding as social science researchers?

Feminist scholars have noted that the value of narratives lies in the emergence of counter-narratives that reveal that the narrators do not necessarily think, feel or act as they are 'supposed to'. Many women's personal narratives unfold within the framework of an apparent acceptance of social norms and expectations, but nevertheless describe strategies and activities that challenge these norms (PNG, 1989: 7). Personal narratives are particularly rich sources because, attentively interpreted, they illuminate both the logic of individuals' courses of action and the effects of system-level constraints within which these courses of action evolve (PNG, 1989: 6). Such narratives can serve to unmask claims that form the basis of domination or they can provide an alternative understanding of the situation (PNG, 1989: 7). The twin questions of memory and truth can be argued to challenge narrative research as an empirical method. However, White (2001) flags the importance of listening to the contradictions, experiences, nuances and interpretations of those facts through oral sources, such as those gathered during an interview process. Mbilinyi argues that the construction of memory and 'fact' during the research process illustrates that a constant process of thinking, shaping and re-shaping occurs in the reconstruction of events (Mbilinyi, 1989: 206). Scholars working on memory as method argue that it provides an opportunity to learn from experiences by ensuring the memories surrounding narratives are not seen as separated from the narrators as things that can be interrogated without them.

6 *Introduction*

Beneath the scraps of memory that have been assembled to create a specific meaning, new paths and possibilities become visible, becoming manifest as contradictions, disharmonies, ruptures, incongruities or inconsistencies.

Structure

This book is anchored around five chapters in addition to the introduction and conclusion. Chapter 1 outlines the conceptual framework that shaped my research. I privilege African feminist analyses to achieve three main objectives. The first objective is to map the trajectory of 'culture' as a political tool deployed by post-colonial African governments to inscribe a gender neutral homogeneous 'African culture' that was inattentive to class, ethnicity or race, religion and gender. I pay attention to the discourses that emerged during this period and sought to define the parameters within which nascent African nations would function. Nyerere's treatise on *Ujamaa* (1968) and Sedar Senghor's movement on *Negritude*, as well as context specific work, such as Kenyatta's *Facing Mount Kenya* (1977) and Oginga Odinga's *Not Yet Uhuru* (1967), also about Kenya, point to the ways in which the idea of a 'national culture' functioned as a mechanism through which new nations were rallied around the perception of a common and often uniting ideology. This ideology was often based on the continuity of the myth of 'untainted African traditions and culture'. Nyerere, for instance, noted the importance of rejecting tribal consciousness in Tanzania as a precursor to the creation of national consciousness (Nyerere, 1967: 38). The effect of this, Mama argues, was the creation of a defensive posture through an erasure of slavery, caste systems and the inhumane treatment of women in traditional cultures (Mama, 1996: 73).

The second objective is an exploration of post-colonial African governments' reconstructions of gendered post-colonial subjects drawing on motherhood, and therefore reproduction, as routes to carve space for women within the state. There was a strategy in some contexts to rewrite women, particularly after their active and often gender non-conforming roles during independence struggles. In other contexts, re-casting women in this way was an attempt to subvert the realities of newly independent nations, which saw migratory patterns shift radically, placing more 'single' women in the cities, thus challenging the 'traditional' notion of the family (see Thomas, 2005). The third objective in drawing on this scholarship is to problematise culturally relativist literature, which uncritically challenges hegemonic Western episteme by, as Lewis (2003) notes, recreating a false unity between African women and men united in a common struggle. These fictions of unity are counteracted by a global development discourse and industry that perpetuates the idea of 'voiceless and helpless' African women who need to be saved. When efforts are made to take context into account and to reconstitute the Western gaze and/or complicity of the colonial discourse, it does so by shaping the need, as Spivak articulates it, 'to save brown women from brown men' (1988: 297). I examine the deficit approach that informs how women are 'introduced' into the state through the narratives of education and the empowerment of grassroots women but also by re-introducing the binaries of modernity, tradition, culture and women's bodies as the sites on which post-colonial masculinities[2] and femininities are reconfigured (see Lewis, 2004; Mama, 1996; Mupotsa & Mhishi, 2008; Thomas, 2005).

Collectively, this body of scholarship offers the theoretical framework for this book through a focus on the nexus between women's bodies, sexuality and the nation, specifically situating the link between the discursive (what is said) and the performative (what is done) with sexuality. The meta-narrative of nationalism and nationhood and its intimate link with the family unit and the woman's body as an axis is critical here. Secondly, the role of 'culture', not only as a strategy by states to 'unify' populations, but also to circumscribe movement, behaviour and interactions by configuring it as a monolithic and unchanging tool is essential to anchoring the discursive. The complicity of the state in shaping narratives around proper masculinities and femininities illustrate how subversion and autonomy, the performativity/discourse nexus are important to 'listening to' and 'seeing' the contestations around gender and sexualities within the nation state. To do so requires paying attention to the interlocking of multiple social and political sites and locations.

In Chapter 2, I examine dominant discourses that have shaped popular debates and scholarship on widow inheritance. The term dominant is used here to describe discourses that emerge as prominent in the context of my research. The material selected for review in this chapter privileges research that analyses widow inheritance from an HIV/AIDS, religion/Christianity, women's rights or cultural anthropological perspective. Even though this chapter privileges material that focusses on widow inheritance amongst the Luo of Kenya, it will also draw on analysis from other contexts, given that the interest here is not on the practice itself but in the discursive production of the practice. My aim is to illuminate some of the key theoretical strands, discursive modes and meta-narratives that have been re-inscribed by such studies. The literature reviewed in this chapter is not historically organised, and neither is it designed to be in conversation with the other since they are produced in isolation both politically and in relation to time. This isolation both frames and grounds the exploration of contemporary, local, popular discourses on widow inheritance, not in terms of expectations around complementarity or even interaction, but in terms of the recognition that these discourses pre-construct the space in which I wanted to find opportunities for the re-theorisation of widow inheritance.

One major tension in accomplishing the core objective of this chapter concerns material offering 'explanatory accounts' of widow inheritance as the only route to engaging the subject. This is a challenge associated with writing about a subject that has already been coloured by hegemonic conceptual frameworks that have rendered it 'harmful', 'backward' and a 'rights abuse', as shall be seen in this chapter. A hyper-vigilance towards this context means a pre-occupation with being misunderstood or rendering simplistic highly complex relational 'conversations'. Such vigilance sees explanations of what 'it is' and what 'it is not' as intersecting with existing theoretical biases. Secondly, the fact that most of the literature reviewed in this section has deployed 'description' as a route into their analysis is also key. There is an obvious political tension between engaging with descriptive texts through questions such as 'what are widowhood rites?', 'what is their purpose and consequences?', and 'what are X's attitudes towards them?' in a study interested in the politics of discourses on widow inheritance. However, I use these texts as one of multiple entry points to unpack the utility of these approaches to understanding widow inheritance. What insights do they yield? What silences do they propagate?

Chapters 3, 4 and 5 analyse the data generated from the field research. In these chapters, I deal specifically with local narratives of the state, nation and 'culture' and how these emerge and are shaped during discussions on widow inheritance. In Chapter 3, I outline the discursive moments emerging during my field work in two major zones. The first is the construction of gendered identities and the second is the discursive construction of sexualities. This chapter pays attention to the ways in which widow inheritance ritualises gendered politics and acts as an avenue to explain and 'resolve' emerging tensions in the political terrain. I explore the themes of location and dislocation, citizenship and perceptions of fixed boundaries that accompany it as established through marital ties and male relatives (father, husband, brother). Chapter 4 focusses on the construction of visible and invisible boundaries as a route to defining 'pure nations'. I explore the notion of gendered citizenship, looking at how this is claimed and contested through widow inheritance. I am interested in the discourse of national identity and how it is intermittently and discursively deployed to include and exclude, to reassert the narrative of community survival and to demarcate the boundaries within which the authenticity of the Luo nation,[3] vis-à-vis other nations, is grounded. Chapter 5 examines the organisation of linguistic practices through metaphors and other linguistic devices as a means of constructing and constraining the performances of gender and sexualities. Drawing on a long trajectory of feminist epistemology (see Cameron, 1998; Lakoff, 1975; Miller & Swift, 1976; Spender, 1980), I analyse how gendered linguistic practices and devices create narratives of permanence and continuity around widow inheritance. Borrowing from Scott's (1987) approach to power and discourse, I analyse the production of counter-hegemonic gendered linguistic practices as resistance.

These chapters illustrate the function of widow inheritance as both a metaphor and a tool for the re-assertion of rigid sexual boundaries. These re-assertions emerged through discourses on gendered subjectivities, the production of a ubiquitous gender neutral 'us' versus 'them', while actively negotiating internal solidarity through the surveillance of women's sexualities. The rejection of non-hegemonic discourses and the performances of alternative sexualities and 'wayward' femininities by women speak to subversive strategies by women and widows, but are also useful for understanding the emergence of non-hegemonic masculinities. I am alert to the embodied nature of these discussions and grapple with the limitations of language, its translatability for purposes of analysis and the need to capture nuances within both embodied and verbal discursive moments.

The book's conclusion draws a link between discourses on widow inheritance as produced in the field work to nation-/state-building processes. I consider three main discursive productions: the first revolves around sexualities constructed through narratives about non-hegemonic femininities; the second is the discursive construction of visible and invisible boundaries negotiated on women's bodies via the vectors of reproduction, disease or taboo; and the third refers to linguistic devices that construct gendered spaces and that are legitimated by myth, taboo and history to entrench a national legacy. These cohere into a broader discourse that effectively questions the conflation between ethnicity and culture. Locating gender and class in the construction of ethnic and political projects reveals how they (gender and class) are deployed to legitimise and discipline the homogeneous collective. This means that ethnicity and culture become moving targets, their discursive utility is essentialised and they become representative of non-unitary constructs.

Notes

1 Ritual cleansers are often younger men who are not related to the widow. They are seen as having commercialised the practice by "inheriting" women for financial gain. Levirates on the other hand are male relatives of the widow's husband who are required to "inherit" the widow. This is discussed in detail in Chapter 2.
2 An important contribution not covered in this book because it was not a focus of the field research is critical masculinities.
3 The term 'nation' is used in the non-juridical sense and draws on early Western political theorising on the origins of the state, as has been variously attempted in most parts of the modern world (see Gellner, 1983). It refers to the scenario where members of a 'nation' share a common identity, and usually a common origin, in the sense of history, ancestry, parentage or descent, in what is commonly referred to as tribe or ethnic group. Though the term 'nation' is also commonly used in informal discourse as a synonym for *state* or *country*, a nation is not identical to a state. This is informed by the fact that a nation, where identities as described above cohere within set boundaries, is non-existent. The idea of a nation state is derived from a unity informed by the political and legal structure of the state.

1 Gender, sexuality and culture

This chapter provides an overview of three major analytical zones that anchor the research in this book. The first section interrogates the absence of gender as a variable in understanding contestations around the 'new African state' in the immediate post independence era. Scholars such as Lewis (2003), Wilson-Tagoe (2003) and Mama (1996) theorize the implications of gender neutrality in analyses of post-colonial state formation. In doing so, they highlight the gendered slippages in the vocabularies of 'culture' and 'democracy' that are key lexicons in analysis of post-independent states.

The second section examines the terms on which women were drawn into the post-colonial African nation/state project. By examining both development and empowerment paradigms, I am interested in deconstructing the lenses that shaped the inclusion of African women in the state. The modernity/ tradition binary emerges as a discursive device used to shape and influence the evolution of gender in the 'modern' nation state, while maintaining the policing and regulation of women's bodies as central to the machinery of nation building. Thomas (2005) and Pereira (2005) and Badoe (2005) suggest that while the contexts and interlocutors may differ, the contested nature of women's sexuality reveal that these are not simply 'private matters'. An analytical approach that ignores women's bodies and gender identity as a site in which both states and nations continually define and redefine themselves is myopic.

The third and final section examines the politics of writing about women's bodies in a period characterised by a range of global concerns, specifically those animated by increased violence against women, HIV/AIDS and women in leadership. In doing so, I examine the legacies and continuities of 'the regimes of "truth" that underpin a political discourse of who can be intimate with whom and in what way and make it a primary concern of the state and community policy (culture)' (Stoler, 2002: 2). These conceptual frames shape the contours of the analysis in this book.

'African culture' and gender

African discourses on 'culture' have emerged out of the historical condition of colonialism, with African cultural theory concentrating on challenging imperialist cultural domination (see Wilson-Tagoe, 2003). The nature of 'culture' as an element of resistance to colonial domination lay in the fact that 'African culture', ideologically, was the manifestation of the material and historical reality of colonised African people (Chabal, 1983: 141). Cabral argued that, 'it was always within the realities termed as cultural that the people found the seeds of challenge, which led to the structuring and development of national liberation movements' (Chabal, 1983: 141). Accordingly, national liberation movements were organised around the expression of 'culture'. Kwame Nkrumah, 'African cultures' saw 'culture' as the core of political revolution noting that socialism lay in the high point of 'African cultures', i.e. the collective ethos (Botwe-Asamoah, 2005: 50). This collective ethos was also manifest on the social level, in institutions such as the clan, which underlay the initial equality of all and the responsibility of the many for the one (Botwe-Asamoah, 2005: 50). This position was also implicit in Julius Nyerere's *Ujamaa* policy, in which he argued that there were no sectional interests in pre-colonial Africa (Nyerere, 1968: 52). Put together, the collective argument was that the production of African culture based on tribe was part of an imperial project, which Africa's national liberation movements sought to re-articulate through the construction of 'national' ideologies (see Chabal, 1983; Nyerere, 1967). Burton (1999) and Stoler (2002) note the centrality of sexuality as a zone and women's bodies as a site through which insecurities related to physical geographical boundaries and internal discord within the false culturally secure colonial set-up were negotiated. They point to the tentative and perhaps contrived nature of cultures created and defined within the colonial set-up, which defined and locked up certain practices and norms as given and assigned them to specific races. Drawing on the intersection of race and gender, Stoler (2002) identifies marginality and fear of disruption of identities underpinning citizenship, nationality and geography – specifically who had access to land and property and who could legally claim these rights.

For African liberation movements, the notion of 'culture' became part of a political process of constructing a distinctive identity through the creation of new knowledge about Africa's place in world history (Wilson-Tagoe, 2003: 25). 'Culture' determined by the exigencies of anti-colonial discourse strengthening the link between 'nation' and 'culture' led to the presentation of culture as coherent and homogeneous rather than as continually contested and renewed (Wilson-Tagoe, 2003: 25). Post-colonial scholars suggest that the contestations around unifying 'culture' and 'traditional' norms in Africa pertain because Africa as an idea and as an object of academic and public discourse has been and continues to remain fraught (Mbembe & Nuttall, 2004: 348; Mudimbe, 1988). Mohanty (2002: 505) asserts that the terms 'Western' and 'Third World' retain a political and explanatory value in a world that appropriates and assimilates multiculturalism and 'difference' through commodification and consumption. References to 'culture' therefore infiltrate discussions and debates in ways that codify and entrench the binary between Africa and the West (Lewis, 2004: 30–1). This argument is picked up in critiques of transnational approaches to feminist scholarship that centre the influence of global discourses on 'other' women. Mohanty refers to it as 'the discursive colonisation of Third World women's lives and struggles through the power/knowledge nexus of feminist cross-cultural scholarship expressed through eurocentric, falsely universalising methodologies' (Mohanty, 2002: 501).

Gender post flag independence

Gender discourses and interventions in post independent African states operated within universalising discourses where 'fictions of authenticity, custom and "the past" worked to bolster patriarchal goals and desires. In doing so as Lewis notes they perpetuated the servitude of women whilst demonising the men and women who reject heterosexist norms' (Lewis, 2003: 1). Nationalist discourse staked out those sexual practices that were nation building and race affirming by marking unproductive eroticism not only as immoral, but also as unpatriotic. Thomas (2005: 175), writing on Kenya, notes how politics of the womb have been crucial to ensuring material prosperity and constructing moral people and communities. While noting the importance of the historical moment in which these discourses are produced, she notes that in Kenya, it has not always been easy to neatly separate issues of land, labour and political control from those of gender, sexuality and reproduction. However, the interface with development discourses in the early 1970's led to a range of essentialist constructions of femininities and therefore gender.

These developmental interventions can be traced to the emergence of the Women in Development (WID) framework that was popularly associated with a wide range of activities concerning women, which donor agencies, governments and NGOs adopted between the 1970s and the 1990s. WID was coined in the early 1970s by a Washington-based network of female development professionals (Tinker, 1990: 30). Based on their experiences of overseas development work, they began to challenge trickle down theories of development by foregrounding the differential impact of modernisation on men and women. Instead of improving women's rights and status, the development process appeared to be contributing to deteriorating their position (Tinker, 1990: 31). The second major influence on WID was the emerging body of research on women in developing countries; the work of the Danish economist, Esther Boserup, was most influential. Boserup's *Women's Role in Economic Development* (1970) challenged the assumptions of the welfare approach to gender by highlighting women's importance to the agricultural economy. Boserup critiqued colonial and post-colonial agricultural policies that had facilitated men's monopoly over new technologies and cash crops and undermined women's traditional roles in agriculture thereby destroying female farming systems (Razavi & Miller, 1995: 11). Consequently, a dichotomy emerged where men were associated with the modern, cash-cropping sector and women with traditional, subsistence agriculture. Relegated to the subsistence sector, women lost income, status and power relative to men. More importantly, their essential contribution to agricultural production became invisible.

Boserup's work was taken up by WID advocates because she offered evidence of a recent past of relative equality for women that could make the case for development assistance to be directed towards women to address gender inequalities, thus also challenging the idea that equality was a Western import (Jaquette, 1990: 61). The singular focus on the consumptive and productive capacity of women to reject the narrative of gender equality as a Western import resulted in an emphasis on efficiency demands as a route to altering their status of powerlessness. Gender re-distributive arguments prioritised women as a group, not because of their needs but due to the targets that could be achieved through their productive labour. Consequently, broader socio-political questions that informed women's and girls' exclusion were muted. The residual effects of these WID approaches can still be felt today with generalised claims about what women's equity can do for states and for development. Razavi (1995) argued then that the cure for Africa's food crisis, child welfare, environmental degradation, and the failure of structural adjustment policies are all sought in women (Razavi & Miller, 1995: 10). The legacies of this approach are evident today. While this greater focus has given women a higher profile in policy discourse, women are expected to compensate for public provisions, even though stringent fiscal policies and mismanagement of resources limit their actual ability to make any shift in structural inequality. Indeed, the unpaid care work debate, that has resurged today in global gender and development circles, was picked up as an unintended effect of the WID approach by Kandiyoti (1988) and Goetz (1994) who pointed to the intensification of women's workloads as the onus shifts to them to extend their unpaid work as feeders, healers and teachers of children to include the provision of basic services to the community. This cushioning of state deficiency in the provision of basic goods and services was an observable trend during the food, financial and fuel crisis in 2015. An AWID study pointed to the increased burden on women through increased care work and increased poverty due to a reduction of decent work, and cuts in wages and jobs. Women's social reproduction roles are called upon without question to cushion economies due the absence of effective infrastructure to deliver education, health, water and food (Craviotto, 2010).

Debates on the role of women in rescuing states from economic underdevelopment are also evident in development funding. On the one hand, funding agencies claim to be setting up self-reliant organisations, yet they are primarily interested in funding short-term projects that would produce quick and measurable results. This has resulted in a development funding discourse that locks those located within it into a tightly regulated set of relations defined by the international marketplace and foreign aid (see Smith, 1997). As Smith argued, contrarian views that suggest that recipients of funding should 'do development' on their own terms are regarded as dangerous because it upsets the balance of power that positions the aid industry as knowers and helpers (Smith, 1997: 229). The impact of neoliberalism on the development sector is illustrated by an AWID (2013) study on the state of funding for women's rights work that points to the systematic reduction of resources towards women's funds and women's organisations. This reduction in funding occurs at the same time as the rise of corporate led programmes targeting girls and women through innovation and entrepreneurship initiatives while at the same time reducing the question of women's freedom to one about individual hard work and economic empowerment, and not about the hetero-patriarchal structural conditions that sustain gender inequalities (Wilson, 2011). The development framing of gender has often overshadowed feminist approaches seeking radical understanding of gender. Lessons learnt from the uptake of gender within 'development' point to the generalities that sustain this work: 'women are the poorest of the poor', 'women do most of the work in African agriculture', 'educating girls leads to economic development' (Cornwall et al., 2008: 1). The NGO-isation of gender has meant that discourses on gender follow global interests and resources. In the 1990s, the HIV/AIDS pandemic and a growing international interest in violence against women, due in part to the increase in violent conflicts on the African continent, opened – albeit problematically – discussions on sexuality. These discussions and the interventions that have followed in their wake have been limited to sexual practices specifically in connection to safety, illness and violence. The articulation of women sexualities through the vectors of disease and pollution, entrench the modernity/tradition binary. Feminist engagement with sexualities that do not re-inscribe these perspectives are positioned as 'a form of liberation from a former victimhood under

Gender, sexuality and culture 15

atrocious African traditionalism or another version of restored respectability' (Mupotsa, 2008: 11). Additionally, the conflation of 'respectable' femininity with social and biological 'mothering' or 'motherhood' is retained as central to the nation, thereby reproducing it as a stable and closed entity (Mupotsa, 2008: 11).

Body politics and sexuality

Feminist analysis of body politics and sexuality illuminates how difference, defiance, morality, purity and dirt re-emerge to validate state-led actions against women's bodies at specific political moments. In Badoe (2005) writing about the "witches camp" in Gambaga explores the narratives of women expelled by their families and communities in one of the four places of exile in the Northern Region of Ghana. Those most vulnerable to witchcraft accusations were widowed women who were forced to move back into their fathers' homes after their husbands had died (Badoe, 2005: 40). Additionally, successful 'single' businesswomen, women without children and women without an adult male brother from the same mother to protect their interests in the extended family were also vulnerable to charges of witchcraft (Badoe, 2005: 41).

Through the Lawal[1] case, Pereira (2005) distinguishes between the legal and normative understandings of *zina*.

> Zina is transgressive according to Sharia criminal law. While the Sharia does not explicitly define zina as transgressive heterosexuality, it is clear from significant elements of its conceptualisation that, for instance, consensual sex between a man and a woman who are not married to one another, . . . that zina involves heterosexual sex and that the source of its transgression is its occurrence outside marriage.
>
> (Pereira, 2005: 52)

Pereira argues that interpretations of *zina* are presented by those whose interests it serves as uniformly applicable under all circumstances and as fundamentally unchanging and unchangeable (Pereira, 2005: 62). Pereira (2005: 75) underscores the significance of history and politics in the interpretation of cultural practices, including practices integral to heterosexual culture. The daily and legal discursive interpretations of *zina* reveal how the surveillance of women, their bodies and their sexualities are sanctioned through civil and religious legislation.

Legislative surveillance also features in the immediate post-independence period in Kenya. Thomas (2005) shows how national debates generated wide-ranging consideration of the state's role in defining and ensuring women's legal rights. Kenyan politicians and the public argued over whether national independence should entail greater autonomy and guaranteed rights for women. Reproduction became the subject of colonial and post-colonial debate and legislative intervention in Kenya because so many people viewed its regulation as fundamental to the construction of political and moral order and proper gender and generational relations (Thomas, 2005: 4). These debates produced diverse political discussions over whether national independence should entail greater autonomy and guaranteed rights for women (Thomas, 2005: 4). The connection between the regulation of reproduction and the construction of political, moral order and proper gender and generational relations is seen in its reflection within state policy objectives (Thomas, 2005: 4). In South Africa, Ratele's analysis on Zuma's rape trial points to the ways in which sexuality becomes a site in which political and legal struggles are re-inscribed and become *de facto* norms. Ratele (2006: 59) continues: 'it is clear that nations, societies and cultures are continually contested and contesting – just as sexual conduct and relations are not "natural" entities, so masculinities and sexual identities and rights are fields of power'. Ratele's work focusses attention on hegemonic and hetero-normative discourses that have coloured analysis on sexuality.

The McFadden–Pereira debate (2003), on the other hand, elucidates the complex terrain (both intellectually and contextually) on which sexuality debates occur. McFadden (2003) argues against the proclivity of feminist work in Africa to engage with what she terms as the 'safer' zones of sexuality. This, in her view, is evident in the overwhelming focus on reproduction (specifically within marriage) and the sex rights discourse as the basis for intellectual and practical work around sexuality. She situates pleasure and choice as a critical part of sexuality by suggesting that the erotic, and the agency associated with claiming it, presents a powerful political and transformative tool. As Mupotsa and Mhishi (2008) note, essentialised categories that position research on sexuality as a liberation discourse, moving away from 'silences' of victimisation and oppression, reveal the characterisation of sites charged with political tension such as reproduction as safe, potentially apolitical zones. Countering McFadden (2003), Pereira (2003) offers the importance of contexts and the heterogeneity of women in Africa as critical starting points for any assessment of 'safety' in approaches. While Pereira does not question the fact that 'silences' exist in approaches to activism and theorising of African women's sexuality, she suggests that the daily negotiation of state, cultural and religious violence by women, with their bodies as a target, offers a potential framework to understand why there is a focus on rights and reproduction in some African contexts.

Continuities: debates on sexuality in Kenya

There are a range of continuities shaping debates on sexuality since 2008 when this research was conducted in Kenya. The tensions that McFadden (2003) noted remain relevant and can also be understood as indicative of intergenerational forms of organising that have developed across the country. Three vignettes are offered here to situate the framework that this book privileges. In 2005, a national constitutional referendum was instituted to begin to close the constitutional reform process begun in the 1990s. The key issues under contention were land ownership, legalisation of abortion in specific cases and the inclusion of Muslim *Kadhi* courts. The Catholic church mobilised its parishioners against the draft based on moral arguments about the sanctity of life and women's responsibility to avoid children out of wedlock. Unplanned pregnancies and choice were immediately linked to the institution of marriage, women's morality, the state and the church's responsibility to secure both. *Warembo ni Yes*,[2] a campaign initiated by *Bunge la Wananchi*,[3] was developed to mobilise young women across the country to vote in the referendum to secure the limited rights on abortion that had been proposed. While the constitution came into being in 2010 with the clause legalising abortion under specific circumstances (threat to a mother's life, rape and mental illness), the policy framework to allow for safe and accessible services for women and girls remain nonexistent. A 2018 decision by the Kenya Medical Practitioners Board barring Marie Stopes International from providing abortion services is indicative of the larger moral veil that clouds the ability to implement legal provisions in a country where unsafe abortions are reported to kill seven women daily (see BBC, 2018; Omboki, 2018). This ban occurred at the same time as public debates about the high rate of teenage pregnancies in Kenya captured public attention due to a United Nations Population Fund estimate that nearly 378,400 adolescent girls between 10 and 19 years of age became pregnant between July 2016 and June 2017 (see Boss, 2018). Absent from dominant public discourse was the place of comprehensive and appropriate sexuality education for school-aged girls and boys. This is an approach that has been championed by women's rights activists as an important way to address teenage pregnancies, unsafe abortions and encourage open and honest conversations on sex and sexuality (see FEMNET, 2018).

On September 6, 2013, Nairobi Governor Evans Kidero was captured on Kenyan television news cameras slapping a woman member of parliament, Rachel Shebesh. Shebesh was in his office to discuss the fate of Nairobi county government employees who were striking over non-payment of salaries. The brazen and vicious nature of the slap shocked most feminist activists, particularly when a few hours later the governor appeared on camera denying that the slap ever happened (see Okech, 2013). What followed were a series of actions that illustrate perceptions of acceptable gendered bodies in public spaces on the one hand, and how femininity and sexuality are mobilised to discredit women in public office on the other. Kidero went to the police station and a doctor miles away from the city centre to file a criminal complaint and acquire a medical report, claiming that he was assaulted by Rachel Shebesh. It was the assault on his sexual organs that triggered the slap. The public discourse generated by the news reports on the issue was split into two. The most dominant voices were those who argued that Shebesh deserved the slap. She was a loud, aggressive woman who needed to be put in her place. She was 'out of control'. A few days later, reports from an aggrieved security guard at her home emerged claiming that she had history of assaulting people. The argument therefore was that violence must be met with violence. A set of false equivalencies were set-up to defend the public assault of a woman leader by a man holding public office. In October, private intimate images of Shebesh with a man who was not her husband were leaked. The intention of these images was to mobilise morality and acceptable femininity to dismiss calls for accountability on an assault that had little to do with whether she was a 'good woman' or not. Under the hashtag *KideroMustGo*, women's rights activists campaigned without success for the governor to step down from office and/or be held accountable for his actions. None of these were achieved, as a private settlement was ultimately reached between the two leaders.

On September 5, 2018, a news item in a local Kenyan daily reported that a university student was found dead in a local forest after being reported missing (Star, 2018). Sharon Otieno's murder became headline news when it emerged that she was the girlfriend of the governor of Migori county, was expecting his child at the time of her death and that the governor's close associate was among the last people to have seen her. *JusticeforSharon*, the hashtag around which Kenyans on social media organised to push for state accountability, revealed the continuing perceptions about femininity and sexuality and morality. The discourse generated around Sharon's murder and therefore young women's sexuality illustrated that a section of Kenyans saw a combination of loose morals and laziness both combined in dating an older married man and opportunism/vengeance (choosing to get pregnant) at the heart of Sharon's problems. The vice chancellor of Rongo University where Sharon was registered argued that students needed 'good morals', referencing young women. The production of immoral youthful femininities constructed as 'out of control', 'lazy' and 'opportunistic' travelled further than the responsibility of older men with socio-economic and political power relative to the young women they preyed on. The problem in the public domain was not the unequal power relationship set up by older men, the problem lay squarely with women whose sexualities and bodies needed to be policed.

The three vignettes in this chapter illustrate the continuities evident in conversations about gender, body politics and sexuality in Kenya. They make the point about the abstraction of gender and sexuality conversations from nation and state-building conversations. Yet, the resultant discourses as shown here are designed to sustain a homogenous vision of masculinity and femininity in relation to the morals and future of the nation. African feminist scholarship situates sexuality within a broader paradigm of political and national power contestations. Specifically, the voices I have privileged in this chapter challenge the conflation of homogenised 'African women' and their sexuality by distinguishing how sexuality is deployed to construct a 'normative African woman'. Non-hegemonic femininities are managed through various surveillance mechanisms to shape 'appropriate sexualities' and gender identities for the service of the state. In a context where identity-based conflict is perennial, a more sophisticated understanding of how gendered identities are forged is critical. This approach is useful for my interest in discourses on widow inheritance. By mapping and analysing popular discourses on widow inheritance, my goal is to uncover robust theorisations about gendered subjectivities.

Notes

1 Amina Lawal was sentenced to death by stoning by a Regional Court in Katsina State, Nigeria for having a child outside marriage. Her sentence was announced on March 22, 2002 and subsequently withdrawn on September 23, 2003.
2 Young women say yes to the constitution.
3 People's parliament – pro-poor social movement historically related to popular social struggles for empowerment and participatory democracy in Kenya since the early 1990s. The movement was started and fronted by people who felt deprived of social justice and decent living conditions: the unemployed, petty traders, squatters and low paid workers who through regular public forums in parks challenged the state privatisation and liberalisation of the economy.

2 Dominant discourses on widow inheritance

> *You can't tell why [widow] inheritance [occurs] because we started seeing it a long time ago, so we grew up seeing it happening. So you must be inherited. If you have children you are inherited so that you do not mess up their future. If you do not have children it [widow inheritance] helps to continue the lineage.*
>
> – Research participant

The term 'widow inheritance'[1] is contested. Scholars solidly within traditions of cultural anthropology (see Ocholla-Ayayo, 1980; Ogot, 1967; Ogutu, 2001) have argued that what happens amongst the Luo people of Kenya is not 'inheritance', but a leviratic union, where a *levir* (a husband's brother) is required by tradition to take on the brother's widow and provide support and protection (Ogutu, 2001: 12). The term is argued to be a misrepresentation of its actual embodiment, noting that attempts to translate the word and process from Dho'Luo lead to a misleading equivalent in English (see Ogutu, 1995). A similar argument is made in respect of the Baganda where 'the notion of "taking over the widow" was necessary and discussed in terms of protecting her from seeking sexual relationships outside the clan to support herself and her children' (Nyanzi et al., 2005: 4). Women's rights activists argue that the term itself is an indication of the violation of women's rights (see CREAW, 2008; HRW, 2003). I work with the term 'widow inheritance' recognising that both scholars and practitioners who deploy the term refer to a similar set of practices that revolve around the death of a male spouse. Additionally, the literature also points to a common understanding that these practices occur within a cultural framework.

Widow inheritance as a 'cultural practice'

The practice of widow inheritance or leviratic marriage is not unique to Kenya or the Luo community. The practice is noted amongst the Baluyia and Joluo in

Kenya, the Batonga in Zambia, the Baganda and Lang'i in Uganda, and in Burkina Faso, Mali, Rwanda, Zimbabwe and Zambia, as well as being prevalent in parts of India and Pakistan. It appears to be predominant in patrilineal and patrilocal societies, where it is expected that the woman will relocate to her husband's home; however, the example of the Batonga – a matrilineal community in Zambia – indicates that this is not always the case (see Malungo, 1999). The studies analysed in this chapter also suggest similarities in the practice across Africa. The Luo (also spelled Lwo) are an ethnic linguistic group living in an area that stretches from southern Sudan, northern Uganda and eastern Congo into western Kenya and the northern part of Tanzania (Ocholla-Ayayo, 1980; Ogot, 1967). The ethnic groups in these areas that speak Dho'Luo include the Dinka, Nuer, Shilluk, Acholi, Lang'o, Padhola, Alur and Joluo of Kenya and Tanzania. Ethnologists, linguists and oral historians document the Luo as part of the Nilotic group of communities who separated from the east Sudanic family of tribes around 3000 BCE (Ogot, 1967). Historians place the area of origin of the Luo in southern Sudan, noting that, more than eight centuries ago, the Luo peoples occupied the area that now lies in eastern Bahr el Ghazal in present-day southern Sudan (Ogot, 1967).

Historians cannot explain why the Luo left this area, but they are known to have moved to nearly all the countries neighbouring Sudan, resulting in many separate groups, with variations in language and tradition emerging, as each group moved further away from their kin (Ogot, 1967). The Luo of present-day Kenya apparently arrived in Kenya between 1500 and 1800 CE. Also known as *Joluo*[2] ('people of Luo'), the traditional system of organising leadership amongst the Luo was through kings (*ruoth*). Some scholars break this down further, noting that '[t]he traditional political structure of the Luo revolves around *ot* (household), *dala/pacho* (homestead), *anyuola* (clan/extended family), *oganda* (nation) and *piny* (conglomeration of nations)' (Ogutu, 2001: 9). The Luo of Kenya have retained a structure called the Council of Luo Elders, led by the *ker*,[3] who is selected upon the death of the incumbent. It is argued that one of the major qualities of the *ker* (always a man) is his knowledge of the culture and traditions of the people and hence his ability to sustain these (Ogutu, 1995). The *ker* is also meant to provide leadership to the people through the Council of Elders, which is a highly contested position, given the diversity and incoherence of 'Luo-ness'. The Council of Luo Elders in many ways remains a political structure that can be abused/misused by Luo politicians. The impact of this institution on the daily realities of Luo people in the country is minimal.

Ties that bind: heterosexual marital bonds

The institution of marriage as the *de facto* means through which non-filial bonds are contracted between men and women, and as the primary means through which heterosexual relations are negotiated and concluded, is taken as a given across all the literature on widow inheritance. The role of heterosexuality as a principle for organising labour and social relations is not troubled in the analysis below. Rather, it is how these relationships should function (or should not function) that comes under scrutiny in discussions on widow inheritance. Scholars such as Ogutu[4] (2001) foreground the institution of marriage, noting that it was entered after an extended process of courtship, often involving go-betweens. The families of both the man and the woman were (and still are) directly involved in the marriage negotiations that culminate in the sealing of the marriage deal through the payment of bride wealth:

> The nature of the negotiation and sealing process meant that once marriage was contracted it was permanent and there was no room for divorce unless the man was impotent. Death did not bring marriage to an end.
>
> (Ogutu, 2001: 11)

It is worth noting the primacy placed on male virility as the only basis for the dissolution of a marriage, implying the possibility of multiple options to test such virility outside the marriage. Conversely, the reproductive capacities of women are a central part of marriage, although there is overall silence both in literature and practice about the 'options' and 'choices' available to reproductively challenged women. The lack of options and emphasis on male virility alludes to the inherent stigma associated with the inability to exercise one's femininity fully. I offer the family structure in the Luo society to understand the historicity and importance of widow inheritance to family ties. The Luo are both patrilineal and patrilocal, which means that inheritance and residence revolves around the man (Cohen & Odhiambo, 1989; Ocholla-Ayayo, 1980; Ogot, 1967; Pala, 1980). As a result, like other Kenyan ethnic groups, a high premium is placed on bearing sons who symbolically carry on the male lineage (Pala, 1980). Ogutu (2001: 10) notes that, through the act and process of consummating the marriage, a woman invariably becomes the wife of her husband, the wife of the household, the wife of the homestead and the wife of the clan. Due to the exogamous nature of Luo marriages, a wife is considered a stranger (*wat ang'iewa*[5]) who needs to be fully integrated into the family. Thus, a premium was placed on the aspiration to become *chi oganda* (wife of the clan), with the least-desired status being that of *chi chwore* (wife of the husband), which is viewed as being selfish and characteristic of urban and economically mobile woman (Ogutu, 2001: 9). *Chi oganda*, per Ogutu (2001: 15), fully accept Luo beliefs and practices, and are Luo wives *par excellence*. Ogutu (2001: 10) notes the right of a Luo wife to full membership of the family, and her right and privilege to have a say in and determine the upbringing and future of her children. However, this right as can be seen below is qualified:

> A Luo woman who respects Luo normative ethics of role and responsibility has cut a niche for herself and would never be marginalized, as one would be led to believe. What is at stake is personality and ability not sex.
>
> (Ogutu, 2001: 9)

Ogutu (2001) takes as given and unproblematic the patrilineal and inherently patriarchal nature of the Luo society through his explanation above of a woman's entry into a Luo home. His explanation of Luo norms does not challenge the fundamental structure of the Luo family. This is based on the provisions put in place for a woman to 'fit into' the said structure. Her agreeing in principle to non-negotiable Luo norms and traditions determine her legitimacy within the extended family. Other scholars have noted that the persistence of these dominating patriarchal structures in contemporary Kenya illustrate the conflict between 'modernity' and 'tradition' (Gwako, 1998: 178). Thus, the centrality of tradition, culture and rituals in enforcing 'law' amongst a people is an attempt to 'resolve' this conflict through a discourse of continuity. This position is reinforced by Ogutu's arguments that directly link the failure to accept 'tradition' with 'modernity' and urbanisation. I will explore the notion of Luo 'normativity' in detail in this chapter.

Becoming a Luo widow

The establishment of the family through heterosexual bonds and an emphasis on heterosexuality organises the immediate family and home and provides the basis for the existence of widow inheritance. Implicit in these analyses is the assumption of hetero-normative gender roles and norms as given. This forms the basis for understanding the function of widow inheritance in maintaining these gendered norms and performances of 'respectable' femininities and masculinities within the larger community. Widow inheritance serves as a framework to contain these norms. Luke argues that widow inheritance arose among the Luo to ensure that adult women remained under the guardianship of a man if their husband died (Luke, 2002: 3). It was further thought that marriage and widow inheritance would reduce female promiscuity, for a single man (the husband or inheritor) is viewed as being able to both control a woman and to satisfy her sexual desires.

Widows were traditionally 'inherited' by one of their husbands' brothers or another male relative (see Kirwen, 1979; Ndisi, 1974). Ogutu (2001) and Potash (1986) explain that the inheritor (*jater*) was usually approached by the widow to request his interest in a 'remarriage'. However, there were also cases where local elders 'appointed' the inheritor, after deciding who could best support her (Ogutu, 2001; Potash, 1986). The inheritor served as a widow's sole and 'legitimate' sexual partner, with such legitimisation arising from his being sanctioned by the elders. Within the new union, young widows were expected to continue childbearing, although any new children bore the name of the deceased husband (see Obbo, 1986; Ocholla-Ayayo, 1980; Potash, 1986).

This new union was not a remarriage. The inheritor served in the deceased husband's place, both physically and sexually (Potash, 1986). Hence, Luo widows are known as 'wives of the grave' (*chi liel*), because the union with their deceased husband is considered to continue (Obbo, 1986; Potash, 1986). Inheritance therefore maintained a widow's obligations to her husband and his family, of which the inheritor was a part, and ensured social and economic support for her and her children. Patrilocal residence rules required new wives to move to their husbands' villages and remain there for the rest of their lives. After the death of their husbands, widows would continue to reside in their deceased husbands' homesteads instead of relocating to the homes of their inheritors (Ndisi, 1974; Potash, 1986).

Potash and other scholars argue that Luo widows maintained a high degree of autonomy, given that they often chose their inheritors and maintained a separate household (Kiragu, 1995; Obbo, 1986; Potash, 1986). Yet in the same breath, Potash (1986) notes that widows were not permitted to choose inheritors outside the clan, who were known as 'strangers'. Ogutu analyses the notion of 'choice' along the same potentially contradictory lines as Potash, arguing that:

> Invoking the rites of Leviratic union terminated the period of mourning. The widow was asked whether she had made any friendship with any of her brothers-in-law during the mourning period. *If she had, her choice was respected, except where there was a cultural impediment. Where she had nobody in mind, the family members, in consultation with her and elderly women in the family, decided on who should take charge of this home.*
> (Ogutu, 2001: 13; emphasis added)

Nyanzi et al., in their study of ritual cleansing in Uganda – *okwabya olumbe* (literally translated as 'bursting the death'), which is a term for a series of rituals within the funeral rites – pointed to a consensus amongst their participants that the marriage was a mutual agreement in which the widow was not coerced to have sexual relations with *bakuza* (levirate guardians) (Nyanzi et al., 2005: 4). However, Ayikukwei et al. (2007), also writing on widow inheritance amongst the Luo, question 'choice' exercised by widows within leviratic unions. They argue that the Luo community believes that a widow who refuses to be cleansed is jeopardising the future of her children by inflicting herself and the entire clan with *chira* (Ayikukwei et al., 2007: 44). *Chira*, as Ogutu (2001: 16) defines it, is a fatal wasting ailment that emerges as a violation of accepted normative behaviour. Ayikukwei et al. (2007: 44) describe it as follows:

> Some clans have this ritual deeply entrenched in their belief system and they dutifully perform the ritual, believing that their children will not lead normal lives. These beliefs create feelings of discomfort and affect the social interactions of the widow with other community members. The widow is socially stigmatized; her status affects marital decisions of close family members who cannot officially marry because of her status.

The fear of the consequences that result from failing to fulfil these rituals is also noted amongst the Batonga in Zambia. Malungo (1999: 46) notes:

> If a person is not 'cleansed', he or she is likely to turn mad, a sickness traditionally known as *cibinde*. To prevent *cibinde*, the traditional rulers and other elderly relatives ensured that a person was cleansed after the death of the spouse. Otherwise, the person who was not cleansed was considered an outcast or unclean and would not be allowed to mingle with other people or go to someone's home, nor reach any public place like wells to draw water.

From both Potash's (1986) and Ogutu's (2001) arguments, the refusal to take on a levir was not an option. They note the tacit provision of 'options' under the guise of choices. This led to a range of circumscriptions in the following ways (see Potash, 1986; Ogutu, 2001). The first concerned the presence of a brother-in-law with whom a widow was meant to develop a friendship whilst mourning her husband. Implicit in this 'option' is the assumption that, in grief, the widow should be alert to her function as *chi oganda* (wife of the clan) and not *chi chwuore* (wife of her husband). If the widow did not fulfil these expectations, the second 'option' would be invoked, and this would involve the elders stepping in to make the decision for her.

Widow inheritance: disembodied and disciplining ritual practices

Durkheim's (1893) model of ritual proposes an interest in social control as a way of understanding ritual. This model draws on a social solidarity thesis that assumes solidarity as a fundamental social requirement and ritual as an indispensable element in the creation of that solidarity. Turner (1969) addresses the role of ritual in dealing with conflict, which suggests that ritual exerts control by forestalling overt rebellion or other threats to social unity. Edelman (1971) describes ritualisation as a means of preserving equanimities within strained social relations by simultaneously escalating and orchestrating conflict in such a way that it has to be and can be resolved (Bell, 1992: 172). For Bell (1992), ritual helps to define certain ways of seeing society as authoritative. It serves to specify what in society is of special significance; it draws people's attention to certain forms of relationships and activity and at the same time deflects their attention from other forms, since every way of seeing is also a way of not seeing (Bell, 1992: 175). Bell notes the importance of understanding ritual acts within a semantic framework where the significance of an action is dependent upon its place and relationship within a context of all other ways of acting: what it echoes; what it inverts; what it alludes to; what it denies (Bell, 1992: 220).

These authors emphasise the notion of control, fear of disruption and resistance as key elements that assist the process of ritualisation, though none of them engage with gender, as a basis of this disruption, and its ritualisation to manage gendered tensions. Bell's position above is useful for understanding the function of widowhood rites in denying and inverting tensions in the community. These tensions can be seen in the role played by widow inheritance in restructuring socio-economic and political power relations disrupted by death. Durkheim's social solidarity thesis offers an additional framework to unpack the role of widow inheritance in constructing social solidarity, where social solidarity is contingent upon the retention of normative gender roles. Ritual as conceptual categories that both comprise and organise knowledge are neither abstract in nature nor independent of the body. Instead, they are directly or indirectly embodied (Bell, 1992: 95).

The transition to widowhood amongst the Luo involves a series of rituals that the bereaved woman is required to observe. These rituals used to last over a year, well after the interment of the corpse. This ritual period has been shortened significantly today, which can be attributed to several factors. These include the failure to conclude marriage related rites such as paying bride price prior to a spouse's death, or the failure to fulfil customary requirements, such as the construction of a house outside the paternal home. Ayikukwei et al. (2007: 38), on the other hand, attribute the shortening of this mourning period to the financial capabilities, age and sexuality of the widow. This is a position that is supported by Ogutu (2001: 14), who argues that the modification of ritual practices is because of 'affluent Luo who seek shortcuts to the restoration process'.

The climax of the mourning rituals for a widow involved two interconnected practices: ritual cleansing (*golo chola*), marked by sex, and *ter*, popularly referred to as 'inheritance'. The ritual sexual intercourse, known as 'cleansing', occurs between the widow and her inheritor. There are many grey areas regarding the interpretation of who was supposed to fulfil what ritual function (see Ayikukwei et al., 2007; Ogutu, 2001). It is argued that the cleanser (*jakowiny*) and the inheritor/levirate (*jater*) were two different individuals. A cleanser was an outsider (not a member of the clan) and the inheritor an in-law (Ocholla-Ayayo, 1996). However, these terms and functions are increasingly conflated, particularly with the professionalisation of the sexual ritual cleansing (*golo chola*), leading to popular interpretations of the 'cleanser' as *jater*. Ayikuwei et al. (2007), and Ogutu (2001) to a lesser extent, are the only studies that map widowhood rites on a gendered community. However, they take as given that rituals are fixed and uncontested for the community, based on their descriptive analysis. In addition, drawing from a discourse that positions 'modernity' and 'tradition' as competing and contradictory forces, they assert historical meaning to widow inheritance thereby positioning its continuity despite shifting forms, which they argue to be 'proof' of its significance to the community. They do not interrogate the interaction of rituals and rites on the social body. For Ayikukwei et al. (2007), the ritualised body is powerless, and ritual is therefore disembodied. On the one hand, the body acts as a vessel on which symbols are marked, and on the other hand, the gendered implications of such mapping remain un-examined. They are instead recognised as normative, natural and uncontested. When the contested nature of ritual through the idea of changing norms is examined, it is understood as being an influence of modernity rather than evidence of resistance, transformation and renewed meaning.

The discursive construction of widow inheritance ritual and rites are inattentive to the role of the rituals in the construction of personhood. The continual production and reproduction of 'culture' and 'tradition' occurs through social practices that are seen to define sociable beings. The centrality of the gendered body to all the rites described above – whether as signifiers through dress, the tying of *okola*, the shaving of hair or as an actual vessel for sexual intercourse – point to it as a site where 'the most minute and local social practices are linked up with the large-scale organisation of power' (Bell, 1992: 202). The body becomes a political field upon which power relations have an immediate hold: 'they invest it, mark it, train it, torture it, force it to carry out tasks to perform ceremonies, to emit signs' (Bell, 1992: 202). As Douglas asserts:

> [s]ince both male and female physiologies lend themselves to the analogy of a vessel that must not pour away or dilute its vital fluids, females are correctly seen as literally the entry point through which the pure content may be adulterated, while males are treated as pores through which the precious stuff may ooze out and be lost, the whole system being thereby enfeebled.
>
> (Douglas, 2002: 156)

A double moral standard is often applied in patrilineal systems to sexual offences where wives introduce impure blood into the lineage through adultery (Douglas, 2002: 156). An examination of how power is negotiated in ritual and how ritual strategies construct distinct forms of domination and resistance is critical to the analysis of the discourse on widowhood rites discussed here. For if, as Douglas (2002: 4) argues, symbols associated with sexual danger – such as those evident in widow inheritance rites – mirror the hierarchy and symmetry that apply to larger social systems, then the same impulse to impose order that brings these rituals into existence can also be supported by continually modifying or enriching them (Douglas, 2002: 5). The only way in which pollution ideas, such as those that frame the need for ritual cleansing, make sense is in relation to a total structure of thought whose keystone boundaries, margins and internal lives are held in relation by rituals of separation (Douglas, 2002: 51).

Scholarship on widow inheritance rites situates bodies as powerless, apolitical and timeless, as merely vessels (whether of men or of women), which are acted upon. This results in the production of discourses that frame women/widows as powerless, and voiceless, and as vectors for 'impurity', i.e. disease and dirt. Consequently, the role of sex-related rites within widowhood rituals have been examined simply as events, which position women and men outside time, and within unchanging gendered dynamics, rather than as power contestations resolved through ritual. The discourse that regards women's bodies as vectors of 'dirt', which need to be cleansed through rituals to remove *chira* and *golo chola*, has also framed research developed at the intersection between HIV/AIDS and widow inheritance, to which I will turn in the next section.

HIV/AIDS: disease as a vector

There is a substantial body of scholarship that chronicles 'harmful traditional and cultural practices' (Caldwell et al., 1989; Packer, 2002;

Dominant discourses on widow inheritance 29

Ssengendo & Ssekatawa, 1999). These studies are premised on understanding sexual behavioural patterns and designing behavioural change interventions to mitigate the spread of HIV/AIDS. Most of these studies are based on psychosocial models, which draw stark and homogeneous binaries between 'Eurasian' models and 'African' ones (Heald, 1995; Nyanzi et al., 2005). Thus, the ideological meanings of race, sexuality, gender, childhood, privacy, morality and nationalism have been rewritten due to HIV/AIDS (Hammonds, 1997: 249). The 'uncontrolled sexuality' of black women continues to be a key feature in the representation of black women in the AIDS epidemic, and consequently silence, erasure and the use of images of immoral sexuality abound in narratives about the experiences of black women with AIDS, resulting in a stigmatised sexuality (Hammonds, 1997: 249).

For scholars and policy makers who seek what are considered effective responses to the HIV/AIDS pandemic, perspectives on culture that emphasise the role traditional cultural institutions and practices can play in re-shaping behaviour that leads to rapid infection rates is privileged. For instance, the Kenyan government's policy on AIDS in 1997, as expressed by the Ministry of Health (MOH), was designed to 'assist society to rid itself of risky practices which are interwoven in culture' (MOH, 1998: 19). Researchers writing from this perspective argue that 'rites and ceremonies . . . are incongruent with the modern way of life and observance of which tend to enhance the contraction, containment and spread of AIDS' (National AIDS/STD Control Programme (NASCOP & MOH, 1998: 11). These 'dangerous cultural practices' include male and female circumcision (or the lack of male circumcision), polygyny and its associated norms of male multiple partnerships and widow inheritance, or the remarriage of widows (Malungo, 1999; NASCOP & MOH, 1998; Ntozi, 1997).

Researchers writing from a behavioural framework argue that, while widow inheritance was traditionally a social safety net for women, in the face of HIV/AIDS, it has become a conduit for the spread of HIV infection. Such research not only begins to construct widow inheritance but also sex as dangerous (see Nyanzi et al., 2005). It furthermore identifies an additional problem, namely widows' vulnerability as an explanation for the existence of a life-threatening practice. Widows are identified as a vector of HIV due to their vulnerability and powerlessness in managing heterosexual marital relations. In the context of the spread of HIV through heterosexual intercourse, researchers such as Sleap argue that there is evidence of a cultural backlash, a call to impose restrictions on women to strengthen traditional culture, thus rejecting so-called Western sexual mores and gender roles (Sleap, 2001: 7). Responsibility is also placed on the state to give 'vulnerable' women agency by implementing effective legislation.

> Among the Luo in Siaya district, women whose husbands have died are expected to observe a cleansing ritual, which has a sexual component before they can be re-incorporated into their society. This ritual endangers widows' lives by exposing them to possible infection with HIV/AIDS. Indeed, the Government of Kenya has failed in its appeals to the Luo to abandon such life-threatening widowhood rituals.
>
> (Ambasa-Shisanya, 2007: 604)

Scholarship that positions widow inheritance as dangerous and widows as victims also seeks to build an evidence base of the dangers of being a woman in this community. This stream of research and accompanying discourse begins to link danger to identity, practice and sex. The Institute of Policy Analysis and Research (IPAR) notes that the practice has a high potential for transmitting the virus (IPAR, 2004: 3). Studies like these have informed the slew of advocacy initiatives (including the National AIDS Control Council [NACC]) calling for a change in 'traditional African culture', calling for the abandonment of 'abhorrent cultural practices' in order to tackle the AIDS pandemic (Kiragu, 1995; NACC, 2000: 19; Ntozi, 1997). This has led to a discourse on change, with resultant public statements issued by community leaders who either condemn or support a ban on widow inheritance (see Nessman, 1999; Kiaye, 1994;). The 'reconstruction' of 'culture' has resulted in the discursive construction of 'modified cultural practices' as a negotiated mechanism to address the conflict between 'modernity' and 'tradition' (see MOH, 1998).

HIV/AIDS has significantly affected the practice of widow inheritance. Consequently, efforts to transform the practice are framed, as argued below, as an attempt to find 'an acceptable balance between the ritual of sexual cleansing and HIV/AIDS' (Ayikukwei et al., 2007: 40). Luo elders have responded by advocating the adaptation of symbolic cleansing that is used by elderly widows (Ayikukwei et al., 2007: 40). In Uganda, Nyanzi et al. (2005: 7) also observe the following:

> Many of these widows reported that they were instructed to sit on the floor in the doorway of their main house with legs stretched outwards. Then a man agnate of their late spouse jumped once or thrice over these extended legs to symbolise the sexual act. Some other widows reported that clan leaders instructed them to provide an inner cloth-belt, spread it on the floor in the doorway and have the male agnate jump over it. It was important that this belt was still warm with the body heat of the widow.

Amongst the Batonga of Zambia, there is the practice of *kusalazya*, which 'chases' the spirits of the deceased from the clan through the woman spouse (Malungo, 1999: 56). Malungo notes that alternate practices of *kusalazya*, which do not involve sexual intercourse, are used because people have realised that this practice is a risk factor in the spread of HIV and, in turn, AIDS. Other scholars writing on the intersection between widow inheritance and HIV/AIDS argue that, contrary to the discourses that construct widow inheritance as the major cause of the spread of HIV/AIDS, this practice could in fact impede the spread of the disease. This position is based on the argument that widow inheritance may localise the infection to a few households, as the infected woman would be attached to a single male (the inheritor) rather than circulating freely amongst men in the community (see Adetunji & Oni, 1999). Adetunji and Oni (1999) argue further that, while the custom is risky for an individual inheritor, the practice prevents the spread of disease to the wider population, noting that a ban on widow inheritance could accelerate the spread of HIV/AIDS. Similar arguments have also been pursued by health practitioners, who assert that, in the contemporary African context, unmarried or 'unattached' women (such as divorced or separated women) are more likely to have numerous sexual partners, as they are often dependent on men for financial support, and these partnerships frequently involve unsafe sexual behaviours (see Caldwell et al., 1989; Doyal, 1994; NACC, 2000; NASCOP & MOH, 1998). They argue that widows who are not inherited and who no longer receive traditional means of assistance are more likely to engage in high-risk behaviour with outside male partners to support themselves economically.

Gwako (1998: 173), basing his argument on the analytical binaries of urban/rural and economically empowered/economically disempowered, looks at the emergence of economically secure and resource-owning widows who become increasingly assertive of their right to make independent decisions about their lives. Based on his work amongst the Maragoli of western Kenya, he argues that widows' decisions are influenced by multiple considerations, some of which are unique to them and thus contradict the monolithic notion of 'the African woman (Gwako, 1998: 174). Widows respond to the conditions in which they live and construct alternatives of subordination through their activities in everyday life and by renouncing the 'cultural prescriptions' that control them (Lamphere et al., 1997: 6, 174). A different discourse on economic empowerment is developing, which constructs women's choices in relation to sexuality and highlights a tension between 'respectability' and prostitution. 'Respectable femininities' are cast as central not only to limiting the spread of HIV/AIDS but also to maintaining widow inheritance as a communal safety net. One such avenue has been through religion or, more specifically, Christianity. While the link between religion as a bargaining tool and HIV/AIDS is somewhat problematic, these two positions are noted as useful for widows to negotiate their way out of possible inheritance.

Religion as a trope

'Saved' or 'born again' Christians or 'modern' people regard widow inheritance as a backward, heathen practice and as the pernicious root of the HIV/AIDS epidemic amongst the Luo people (Prince, 2007: 85). Perspectives that privilege religion as an explanatory tool see widow inheritance as a backward, heathen practice and at the root of the HIV/AIDS epidemic amongst the Luo people (Prince, 2007: 85). Widow inheritance is seen to compromise modern and Christian identities, with the HIV/AIDS pandemic constructed as the result of traditional, heathen, sinful ways. Widow inheritance is therefore regarded not only as sinful, but dangerous, as it spreads disease and death, but those who follow Luo tradition and are also Christian and see no conflict between Luo and Christian ways (Prince, 2007: 86). A tension is observed between religious and cultural 'norms', where the idea of sex as a pathway to restitution through ritual cleansing is cast in a suspicious light. It is perceived as antithetical to the sensibilities of 'saved' Christians (Prince, 2007: 85). This tension provides a safety net for widows who argue that religion offers a way out of widow inheritance. However, scholars such as Ogutu sees no tension between widow inheritance and religion. In fact, his long treatise on wife inheritance entitled *Ruth*[6] (Ogutu, 2001) is based on the distinction between Ruth and Orpah in the bible. Ogutu begins his treatise with a quote from the bible: 'Religion that God our Father accepts as pure and faultless is this: to look after orphans and *widows in their distress and to keep oneself from being polluted by the world*' (James 1: 27; emphasis added). He goes on to trace Jesus' ancestor King David as a product of a leviratic union.[7] The purpose of this elaborate introduction is not lost to the discerning eye, for it seeks to affirm the sanctity of the practice and illustrate the 'great people' who have emerged from such lineages, in addition to confirming its Christian foundations. In this regard, while the problem of HIV/AIDS is acknowledged, its associated sickness and death appear to have little to do with the practice:

> The death of today is a consequence of people leaving traditions, which brings confusion to social relations and results in sickness and death and that the only way to avoid personal, social and cultural crisis is by following the rules. Tradition is something one must return to in order to identify and water your roots.
>
> (Ogutu, 1995: xi)

The discourse on 'Luo ways' (*chike*) is situated in an oppositional discourse constructed by historical missionary and Christian opposition to certain Luo cultural and social practices that introduced polarity between 'Luo ways' and 'Christian ways'. Prince suggests that this tension provoked nostalgia amongst some Luo for what have come to be imagined as the ways of the past (Prince, 2007: 101):

> Within the framework of codifying traditions, custom and tradition (*chike*) are constituted as unchanging, the content and form of Luo tradition has been shifting as is the case with other inventions of tradition in African societies. The shift towards the law like application of *chike* and the focus on *chira* with its emphasis on sexual conduct and women's mobility transforms *chike* into men's rules regulating women's conduct (although women can and do use these rules strategically too).
>
> (Prince, 2007: 101)

The creation of *chike* serves three main functions. The first function is to create a distinction between the 'old ways' and the 'new ways', where applications of religion as recognising inheritance are drawn from the Old Testament. The second function is to embed customary law, which in most countries in Africa, including Kenya, exists concurrently with common law. However, the Kenyan legal system gives primacy to the civil law whilst acknowledging customary law. In addition, international rights instruments automatically become law once ratified by the government. This means that international legal provisions on women's rights become part on local jurisprudence. It is at the intersection of these three sets of laws that contestations on culture generally – and widow inheritance specifically – sit. The third function locks women into a gendered power hierarchy that controls their bodily autonomy and sexuality integrity. The third discursive and practical tension has been utilised by women's rights activists to challenge the legality of widow inheritance and to ground a contradiction between common law that responds to 'current' realities and customary laws that responds to 'old ways'. The fact that women's rights discourses are anchored within international rights instruments as a basis for negotiating claims to the state has meant that one of the active sites for advocacy has been within the law (see Human Rights Watch, 2003; Ntozi, 1997; *New York Times*, 2004; Owen, 1996; Sleap, 2001; Wortel, 2004). The inability of women to claim rights and/or assert control has been viewed as discriminatory and has thus been used as a basis to dismiss one set of laws rather than demystify the reality of these binaries. I will now explore in some depth what I refer to as a women's rights perspective on widow inheritance.

Women's rights and widow inheritance

The definition of women's agency within these texts is predicated on survival, rather than on recognising active processes of subversion and transgression. These approaches reinforce agency based on survival and existential questions (see Mikell, 1997), and furthermore take heteronormativity as a given and as an organising force that cannot be destablised. The class dynamics within these studies also silence and de-legitimise the existence of an urban Luo widow who negotiates the same dynamics as her 'universally oppressed' poor and rural counterpart, through the construction of disenfranchised widows as poor and rural. Studies that foreground empowerment and developmental paradigms that include women as able members of the society do so from a belief of the direct correlation between economic wealth and choice. Several routes have been used to construct this engagement. All of them are based on human and women's rights language, but each one focusses on a different set of rights as key to holding the state accountable. The first explores the intersection between widow inheritance, HIV/AIDS and access to land. In this instance, two issues of concern emerge: the first is that widow inheritance renders widows susceptible to infection with HIV/AIDS and that it is thus necessary to do away with this practice. The second, however, takes it as a cultural reality that widows may find difficult to challenge and therefore asserts the need to protect the rights of widows to inherit their husband's property. The property rights discourse draws a strong link to the 'benefits' associated with vesting such inheritance in women – beyond the fact that they are caregivers and therefore carry more responsibility in the home. It also offers greater dividends for micro and in turn macro economies. Embedded in this discourse is the use of economic sustainability and development aspirations of the state as a basis for negotiating with the state around the incoherence between customary and common law. Wahome argues:

> The social construction of gender is impacted negatively by creating inequitable property rights and participation in the economic activity. No wonder the same biased lines continued to inform or influence development policies and programmes in the independent states, thereby throwing women into insignificant roles in the political arena and new market economy. To correct this situation, one must address the changing roles in modern society, international human rights instruments[3] and the contribution of women to economic development.
>
> (Wahome, 2001: 3)

Implicit in this debate is the assertion that the spread of HIV/AIDS is curtailed when women have viable economic opportunities that do not predispose them to engaging in risky sexual patterns to survive. Therefore, a logical conclusion is drawn between empowering[8] women and their refusal of widow inheritance. This logic is produced by a modernity discourse.

In responding to the tensions between customary and common law, the institution of marriage has come under scrutiny. One of the most recent engagements with the institution of marriage occurred in 2009 with the reintroduction of the 2007 Marriage Bill. Since 1981, the Kenya Law Reform Commission had made continuous efforts to amend the existing Marriage Law that had been promulgated by the British in 1967. This legislation was rejected by the post-colonial African government as being inattentive to African culture and tradition and was therefore not passed (see Thongori, 2009). Subsequent efforts by the Kenya Law Reform Commission led to the development of the 2007 Marriage Act, which sought to harmonise 'culture and tradition' and 'modernity' insofar as they affected the institution of marriage. The Marriage Act recognises both monogamous and polygamous marriages. However, those married under monogamous marriages cannot contract polygamous marriages. Further, those who have chosen polygamy cannot contract monogamous marriages. In addition, the ability to register customary marriages entrenches these forms of marriage in law, which means that they are not reliant on the discretion of a judge or customary leaders. The Marriage Act also recognises marriages by cohabitation and allows for their registration. It has been variously condemned for granting women 'too many rights', such as the right to specify at the time of the marriage whether or not her husband may choose to take future wives. The version of the bill reintroduced in March 2009 eliminated a wife's right to stipulate monogamy or polygamy.

Understanding the legal framework within which marriage in Kenya is partially contracted is useful for understanding the approaches that have been adopted by women's rights activists around practices that are predicated on marriage, such as widow inheritance. The questions of choice and rights for women have been high on the agenda because of their absence within the legal dispensation under which most marriages are conducted. The inability to enforce such rights is underscored by the existence of competing and acknowledged laws governing customary marriages in addition to the normativity of common law marriages based on Christian or Islamic doctrines. However, these marriages are almost always accompanied by customary arrangements whose role is to legitimise them for the family and the clan. As such, bride wealth becomes a mechanism for legitimising common law marriages, given that such familial/marital relationships are negotiated in the realm of 'custom'.

Re-casting the tensions in legal systems as an indicator of a tension between modernity and tradition, and its resolution within 'development', has led to a discursive link between the inconsistency in the law to the State's obligation to citizens and its aspirations towards development. Sweetman (2008) argues below for naming women's centrality to the development agenda by explaining the consequences that a non-rights terrain could create for the economy of a country. She argues that the HIV/AIDS pandemic acts as a useful terrain within which to begin to campaign for the rights of women to inheritance and property as the custodians of future generations (Sweetman, 2008: 3–4). She notes:

> Development needs women's equal property rights. Among other things, they increase agricultural productivity, ensure more secure access to services, and provide incentives and ability to invest. By improving women's bargaining power within marriage, ultimately promoting property rights using development arguments creates a virtuous circle in that it ultimately challenges ideas and beliefs about women being 'junior partners' in marriage and enables them to assert equality with men.
>
> (Sweetman, 2008: 3–4)

The link made to rights, empowerment and access to resources via the law, while useful, leaves out various zones within which power and legitimacy are negotiated. The debates on sex and sexuality, when they have occurred, have been automatically linked to the discourse on HIV/AIDS, while choice and rights have been associated with property and inheritance rights. This approach to defining sexual rights as state obligations, Correa (2002) argues, is openly aligned with a political pragmatic perspective. As such, sexual rights become a discursive strategy to enhance the potential of individuals in relation to the state and other agents, and the law itself, thus creating multiple spaces in which their own identities and the meanings of these rights can be refined. In doing this, women's rights activists have not posed an adequate challenge to the charge of 'modernization' created by the discursive 'codification' of norms and traditions, which have successfully and opportunistically been deployed by the state.

The well-documented case of *S.M. Otieno vs Wambui Otieno* (see Odhiambo & Cohen, 1992; Ojwang & Mugambi, 1989; Stamp, 1991) highlighted the ways in which a legal process was used as an avenue to 'codify' Luo norms and traditions, through 'expert testimony' even where they contradicted normative applications of the law. The courts have deferred to customs and customary law because of the absence of corresponding provisions in common law, such as over rights to a body for burial, as was the case here. Instead, the 'modernity/tradition' binary has been re-asserted by women's rights advocacy initiatives as the basis for claiming rights; bureaucracies and 'cultural custodians' use this same basis to counter rights claims. The fact that 'modernity' and 'tradition' have in fact been created by the dominant ruling elite and associated interest groups is left unchallenged in the mainstream. To challenge it would require a move beyond identity through the uptake of collective agency against patriarchy (Mama, 2001: 17). This position assumes the plausibility of a women's movement that supersedes ethnic identities as a basis for resource mobilisation in a context where multiple identities are continually formed and redefined. However, it underplays the power of the ideological interference offered by 'culture', 'tradition' and 'modernity' as binaries that have been deployed by the state and its agents to destabilise the coherence of other identities. It also underestimates the ways in which gender and identity (in this context ethnic) discourses are deeply naturalised even within the strategies deployed within women's rights activism.

Conclusion

The scholarship reviewed here offers a range of discursive strands. There are three main commonalities. The first conceptual commonality in the literature examined is the tension between continuity and change that is pursued through the idea of 'modernity' and 'tradition'. It is underwritten by a generational narrative that constructs a sub-discourse of 'interruption/ change' through age (in the case of young widows), education and access to different environments. For cultural anthropologists, 'change/interruption' is reflective of modernisation and influenced by class dynamics (education, economic empowerment) and youth, where hyper-sexuality is constructed in opposition to 'respectable femininity'. The notion of access as constructed within the discourse of 'change' is also central to the women's rights and empowerment discourse that situates change within a legal terrain as one that promises a future where development gains for all can be achieved. This discourse reinforces the idea of susceptibility of 'culture' to an image of widows as 'generally trodden upon, poor and least protected as their lives are determined by local, patriarchal interpretations of "tradition", "custom", and religion' (Mwenda, 2007: 1)

Within the discourse of 'empowerment', the possibility for 'choice' is only read under the hue of associated threats and exclusionary tactics that are largely based on the risks associated with losing property, including land. Access to and control of land is presented as a major contestation with economic resources seen as allowing women to lay claim to land and its associated benefits. This approach belies the importance of both geographical and psycho-emotional memory associated with 'ancestral' land. It is also anchored within a developmental paradigm that sees a correlation between gender inequality and unequal property rights as a hindrance to economic development, since it contributes to low agricultural production, food shortages, underemployment and rural poverty.

The empowerment approach is also anchored within a vibrant movement for legal reform that challenges the existence of dual and sometime triple legal systems (customary, Islamic and statutory law). The move towards legislative reform is informed by a connection made between HIV/AIDS, vulnerability to violence, 'culture' and social subordination. To reduce the vulnerability of women and girls to HIV/AIDS, an empowerment approach promotes expanded treatment, care and prevention programs for women and girls, and support programmes that improve access to justice and legal representation in Africa, including in divorce and inheritance cases (see CREAW, 2008; HRW, 2003; Oxfam, 2008). This discourse draws on early human rights activism that foregrounded the importance of drawing violence against women out of the private sphere into the broader human rights agenda. Empowerment at the grassroots level, legal reforms and interdisciplinary approaches were critical to this agenda (see Bunch, 1995; Chapman, 1990).

Common to both the empowerment discourse and the 'cultural' discourse is the deployment of the modernity/tradition binary as the core basis of analysis. Where religion (Christianity), economic empowerment and choice are predicated on urban exposure and access as features of the 'modernized' woman, constraint and acquiescence to culture are perceived as features of the 'traditional' woman, which the 'cultural' custodians deem to represent 'respectable' womanhood. A second commonality involves the tools and acts of subversion. Here religion and economic mobility feature highly. Scholars such as Nyanzi et al. (2005) see this as a strategy of subversion deployed by various women to respond to their realities and therefore as evidence of women's agency. Using the lens of economic empowerment, Gwako (1998) sees it as a bargaining strength that most widows use to avoid being inherited, arguing that the lack of a strong economic base from which to bargain can influence the perception of choices. Gwako's analysis is alert to the questions of agency and subversion by looking at the ways in which widows make meaning of the practice and become active agents within it. He is equally alert to development discourses – feminist and otherwise – that influence how widows engage with issues around widow inheritance and property ownership.

The bargaining theory model that he uses provides a useful lens through which the transformation of this cultural practice can be analysed. However, the restrictive association with financial resources limits the scope within which 'bargaining' and 'gain' can be analysed further. Inconsistencies emerge, given the construction of women as passive actors within the practice while at the same time recognising their power, which in this instance is exercised through prescribed activities within widow inheritance rites. On the one hand, Ogutu (2001) and Ayikukwei et al. (2007) position widows as liable to being ostracised for failing to conform to normative Luo ethics, thus rendering them unable to challenge some of these positions. At the same time, they position women as sexual beings who seek the services of professional cleansers due to their economic mobility. The location of women as licentious, hot-blooded women unable to control their sexual desires is juxtaposed against 'normative cultural ethics' that should act as a bulwark against such 'largesse'. The inability of this tension, as well as the correlations among myth, economics and power, to deconstruct this contradiction in a meaningful way, leaves this analysis open to questioning, particularly in relation to the position of women, but also with regard to an awareness of the external dynamics that are bound to shape any process of 'developing a culture'. Such interfaces or sites of liminality present opportunities for unpacking not only zones of resistance, disengagement and engagement, but also spaces for uncovering the emergence, development and assertion of certain meta-narratives as 'normative Luo culture and ethics'. The third commonality concerns the correlation between women and contagion, which is an area that remains markedly under-problematised. Two main tensions emerge through the analytical connection made between widow inheritance, contagion and women as vectors for disease. It is these tensions that frame the intervention that my research offers

The first tension is seen in the location of HIV/AIDS as positively transforming popular understandings of widow inheritance. This is seen within the discourse developed by national health institutions, which suggest the value of the practice in localising the spread of HIV due to the presence of only one inheritor. Doing away with the practice would, they contend, inadvertently open widows to multiple partners, and in this instance, they single out younger women as a high-risk group. The political economy of the body is articulated through an argument predicated on survival, albeit in a less nuanced manner, that barely engages with the subtext of women's bodily autonomy and women's ability to exercise conscious choice. Implicit in these positions is the imperative to control and survey women's sexual encounters through a practice such as widow inheritance.

The second tension emerges through the discursive construction of widow inheritance as a rejection of 'Luo norms'. The arrival of 'new death' – HIV/AIDS – is a consequence of a retreat from 'cultural norms'. This discourse also positions urban and economically empowered widows as responsible for this deviation. They are constructed as promiscuous and the choices they exercise as risky for the community. This contrasts with 'respectable Luo women', who through their participation in widow inheritance rites safeguard the community. The need to counter the perception of all widows as sexually free can be used to explain the function of church and religion as a mechanism to restore respectability to widows who choose not to be inherited.

The failure to problematise contagion, women as vectors of disease and the underlying power dynamics within ritual practices is a big gap across all the literature reviewed in this chapter, particularly in Ayikukwei et al. (2007), who locate ritual and symbols as the theoretical basis for their analysis. The centrality of the woman's body as a ritual body beyond a sexual vessel is not scrutinised. As Jackson and Scott (1996: 26) note, the material appropriation of women's bodies and the cultural signals accorded to sexuality are interrelated. Therefore, one cannot concentrate on the appropriation of women's bodies without paying attention to the cultural meanings mapped onto these bodies. Douglas' thesis on sex pollution is useful for thinking about widow inheritance, for it unpacks the centrality of sex-related rituals and rites and locates them within an understanding of purity vis-à-vis pollution or contagion. By situating the body and the embodiment of ritual as part of a process of re-inscribing and contesting power, it provides a framework to examine widow inheritance as a disciplining device.

Notes

1 Wife inheritance is also used interchangeably with widow inheritance.
2 *Joluo* are also known as *Jaluo* (singular).
3 *Ker* means 'the most revered one'.
4 I draw extensively on the work of Gilbert Ogutu, who has written widely on widow inheritance and traditional institutions of the Luo. As the former secretary general of the Luo Council of Elders, his views as a key scholar in this regard are important.
5 A direct translation of this term would be a 'bought relation'. However, the nature of this term is problematic within the Luo language due to its overt meanings of sale, exchange and negotiated property.
6 I must emphasise that the dedication page in this publication identifies his mother as a so-called Ruth in his father's home and that this work is dedicated to past, present and future products of leviratic unions (Ogutu, 2001: 4).
7 "Ruth, who married Boaz; who gave birth to Obed; who was the father of Jesse, the father of King David; who was the ancestor of Jesus" (Ogutu, 2001: 4). The marriage of Ruth and Boaz is interpreted as a leviratic union and is seen to fall within Jesus' family tree.
8 The concept of empowerment was adopted by development agencies after the Beijing Conference (1995). The Beijing Declaration (section 13) presents women's empowerment as a key strategy for development: 'Women's empowerment and their full participation based on equality in all spheres of society, including participation in the decision-making process and access to power, are fundamental for the achievement of equality, development and peace'.

3 Widow inheritance and gender identity

In contexts where ethnicity forms a basis for the contestation of state resources, it is necessary to examine critical cultural practices that derive their justification from procreation, regeneration and the maintenance of a 'pure' lineage (see Douglas, 2002; McClintock, 1995; Stoler, 2002; Thomas, 2005). In my research, I was attentive to the lived and discursive production of gender, sex and sexuality during discussions on widow inheritance rites and its intersection with the nation-/state-building project in Kenya. The analysis in this chapter is framed by two concerns. The first concern recognises the disjuncture between the articulation and portrayal of women's agency in literature on widow inheritance reviewed in Chapter 2 and the field data. My entry into the field was based on an interest in the participants' experiences of widow inheritance. However, it is the discourses produced during the narration of experiences rather than the narratives themselves that this chapter analyses. This approach re-affirmed the importance of examining the discursive reconstruction of 'culture', women's agency and embodied practices as critical lenses through which to understand widow inheritance.

The second concern that framed my field research was the political debates and processes in the country, which I argue contributed to the construction of 'new' discourses on nationhood and on being Kenyan. I conducted my field research in the aftermath of the post-election crisis in Kenya in 2008, which left people displaced and resulted in an African Union-led mediated coalition government. This political moment had implications for gendered bodies and citizenship, and re-cast the function of widow inheritance. The resurgence of 'culture' and ethnicity as identities from which self-location occurred heightened the need to 'defend the tribe' and associated markers of ethnicity. Consequently, debates about women's sexuality in general and reproduction specifically came into sharp focus. I recognise that the views I will illuminate in this chapter may have always been present in discussions about widow inheritance. However, I suggest that hitherto latent and covert views became overt and politicised during that time. The political moment, in my view, offered insight into how moments of crisis in Kenya's history have contributed to the resurgence of debates on widow inheritance. These moments link widow inheritance to nation-/state-building aspirations and agendas.

Politics of gender

I arrive at a homestead in Ahero to conduct a focus group discussion with an elderly group of participants. My host is not present. Some of the focus group participants have arrived and the daughter-in-law ushers us into the house. An elderly man who was probably in his eighties informs us that we cannot sit in the house when the head of the home is not around. He instructs the daughter-in-law to assemble chairs and a table under a tree. We make our way to the tree. All the men take positions around the coffee table, with only three of the women, who were residents of the home, joining us around the table. The rest of the women who join the meeting later sit on the ground outside the initial circle. Some men come later and find space within the circle around the table and position themselves accordingly. All men sit in places where they have direct eye contact with me, whom they had identified as the reason for the meeting. As we settle down a man who looks like the oldest in the group (and the same man who initiated the move to the tree) states:

BOYA: [man participant]: Dhako ok nyal chwoyo kom ni oluongo bura [Direct translation – 'No woman can put a chair down and claim that she is calling a meeting'.] In fact I am only sitting here because you are a visitor but under other circumstances I would not attend a meeting called by a woman.

The focus group discussion begins, with the establishment of who is in charge and a clear delineation how gendered politics play out. In using this moment to refocus the discussion on widow inheritance, which was my interest, I turned to an elderly lady:

AWINO: I wanted to ask my grandmother here, what do you think about the fact that women cannot call meetings, in essence they are not in charge of the affairs of their home?
DELPHINA [WOMAN PARTICIPANT]: It is a big embarrassment if a woman calls a meeting without a man. We were three women married to one man. I was the eldest and did not want to be inherited, because I was

saved [i.e. in Christian terms], but was forced so that I could open ways for my younger co-wives. This man seated here inherited me. I stayed for six months without going to church because I had transgressed and only returned afterwards. My in-law is still with me today.

AWINO: Tell me a little bit about this embarrassment you talk about in terms of women being in charge of their homes.

DELPHINA [WOMAN PARTICIPANT]: A woman cannot call a meeting when there is a man. What power do women have? Women have no say before their husbands; men have powers. A woman cannot serve any alcoholic drink.

DIXON [MAN PARTICIPANT]: Yes, if she had power she would do these things, for example, build a house on her own, but since she doesn't, a man [participant uses the term '*dume*' – a bull] must be present to release her. You will find that her husband left her a house, which was almost collapsing. Nobody could agree to construct it for her, thus forcing her to look for her in-law to inherit her so that they could do it with him. A woman cannot point out to her son where he should build his house; only a man can do so. Then it would reach a point when this boy will want to marry and in effect want to pay bride price. It is only the man who can release the cows for dowry.

DIXON: You see, these women are imported; the original man of the land has the power; where she may have had power, we had already imported her from there.

As illustrated above the politics of gender emerge in discussions on the role of widow inheritance through the construction of femininity and masculinity. These discursive constructions are framed through notions of what men and women should do (i.e. their roles), what women are expected to wear, how women and men are expected to behave and how interactions between individuals of the opposite sex are surveyed. Gender and its performance via heterosexuality cannot be understood as purely a sexual interaction as its ordering function goes beyond the domestic sphere into other macro zones, thus legitimising some performances of gender and sexuality as correct and others as incorrect. In this regard, what constitutes the public and private sphere becomes the first distinction through which the politics of gender manifests in discussions on widow inheritance. Feminist scholars have debunked the public/private dichotomy. The private sphere is a space where women continuously negotiate both power and powerlessness and must be examined critically (see Rubin, 1975; Yuval-Davis, 1997). As Butler notes, 'our most personal acts are, in fact, continually being scripted by hegemonic conventions and ideologies' (1990: 272).

In discussions with the participants, the public domain is the site where decisions are made on behalf of family. These decisions include the negotiation of familial contracts, such as those surrounding marriage and death, as well as matters related to developments in the home, such as the construction of a house. This is also the sphere where disputes are resolved. This zone remains within the purview of the male members of the home (who also include the sons of the widow). The location of activities, such as the construction of a house and convening family meetings, is limited to men, irrespective of women's vested interests and/ or control of relevant resources. It is important to note that the construction of the house concerns the practicalities of it, specifically on which land it sits. Public space is arrogated in a gendered manner, with widow inheritance providing the framework for it. Women's powerlessness in the public domain is constructed alongside the centrality of a man's roles and responsibilities, such as the reference to the presence of a *dume* (bull) during the construction of a house. Of interest are counter discourses that emerge about the public and private as distinct spheres reinforced by widowhood rites.

The exercise of power through the performance of 'public' roles – in this instance, the construction of a house – is at best fraught. This is evident in an examination of what allows men to arrogate power in the public domain. An analysis of women's personal narratives[1] reveals that in instances where women are the holders of financial resources, men become *symbols* of power and not actual power holders. The importance of this symbolism as a manifestation of 'actual power' cannot be dismissed, for it reinforces gendered ideas about the embodiment of power and authority. The development of the discourse of symbolic power offers an alternative lens, one that situates power in different centres, exercised to different degrees, by different actors and at different moments. The excerpt below from a focus group discussion with women who were widows, or were previously widowed, illuminates the shifting nature of power and the contested nature of men's symbolic power.

AUMA [WOMAN PARTICIPANT]: My sister got married after her husband died, so she left her two children with their grandmother to look for money. She ended up building her own home. She had a friend from Migori who helped her build the house, i.e. he stood as the man, and her son is alive and well. So I think you could just build your own home without getting inherited.

[Laughter and interruptions]

TERESA [WOMAN PARTICIPANT]: But she had a man friend. . . .

AUMA: But technically she did not have a man – this was just a friend. Give me a chance, let me say something: you can build a house without a man, but when you are young, that is a different story.

PLISTER [WOMAN PARTICIPANT]: Today's inheritance is like business because if you don't cook nice meals to [for?] the man he will leave you. It has also led to prostitution because he might be with you and he has others outside. In today's inheritance, you can bring even different tribe to inherit you. You might be working with a Kikuyu man and when your husband dies, you can decide to bring him home, build a home for you and then go back to where you work. This is prostitution and is very common with very many young women today.

RUTH [WOMAN PARTICIPANT]: I agree with her, my husband died and I was inherited. I stayed with him for 6 years but this fellow all he wanted was to eat well and yet he has come home with nothing. He has never done anything related to rituals; I do my work alone. My kids don't even recognise him because they understand their father had already died.

The symbolic nature of power and authority vested in a man's roles, and which subsequently allow for the arrogation of power in the public domain, is highlighted in the above exchange. The participants above debate the technicalities of whether the woman in question had to have a man present to construct her house. Secondly, the meaning of having a man can be symbolic as made evident in Auma relating her sister's narrative. The symbolic presence, she argues, 'allowed' for the fulfilment of a practical need – the construction of a house. The other participants, while recognising this, complicate the idea of the absence of a man by arguing that, technical or not, his presence was important. They imply that, even if Auma's sister subverted the idea of a man's presence during house construction by potentially avoiding an accompanying and perhaps expected sexual relationship, the subversion only occurred through an affirmation of a man's centrality to the process.

In addition, male power is also re-constructed through an instrumentalisation of the *ter* process. This contestation is produced through narratives that highlight the transactional nature of the *ter* relationship. Both Plister's and Ruth's assertions highlight not only on the fact that the *ter* relationship is reliant on the construction of 'safety' through comfort but also in the fluidity of the boundaries[2] associated with who can be a *jater*. The fluidity in boundaries evident in the choices of non-Luos as inheritors and the failure of *joter* to fulfil expected roles renders men's roles irrelevant. It is clear that perceptions of where real power lies are at play in these excerpts. Secondly, the processes that accompany or that are created to affirm this authority are also under consideration. In response to the first, perceptions of power are created through insistence that a designated man must be 'present' upon the death of a spouse for certain activities to be performed, such as the construction of a house, the negotiation and payment of a dowry or the convening of any other general family meetings. Such insistence on presence situates men as power holders within the family. As a result, power is embedded in the processes they are associated with and authority becomes vested in gendered roles. The fact that these processes (such as the construction of a house, larger family meetings and bride price negotiations) are performed in the public domain, outside the household, lends further legitimacy to the place and position of men as public actors.

The power that widows hold upon their husband's death through being in sole control of family resources and thereby asserting their role as primary decision makers is subverted through hegemonic discourses about men, public space and gendered roles. However, this does not prevent the emergence of a counter discourse, one in which women subvert the importance associated with men by constructing a symbolic male presence, as suggested previously by Auma. The contestations,[3] around whether this form of subversion is transformative or not, are raised by the other participants in the group, who note that the significance of men to the process (house construction) is still affirmed and that power is thus not fully given to a woman in her own right. This engagement with power was different among a slightly younger group of women who debated the question of symbolic versus real power. The discussions pointed to age as a variable that located some forms of subversion as beyond the realm of her possibility. Culture and widow inheritance in this instance are only the route through which a woman's own legitimacy – and, indeed, her femininity – can be re-embedded after her husband's death. The debates around power and symbolism offer insight into how a woman's legitimacy in the home is entrenched. Legitimacy is important to this analysis, because widow inheritance is noted to be a framework for continuity; consequently, some performances of gender are a route to establishing citizenship. The following excerpt illuminates this point:

JULIUS: Finally, someone who was old, like this mama here, you would simply leave your coat and that would be it. You were now the head of the household and if there were meetings, you would be called to chair those meetings.

KEZIA: When I was young in our home, my grandfather died. Our home was big and my grandfather had many wives. Upon his death, when my grandmother was going to the farm, she would sing dirges and something was tied in her arm. Her hair was shaggy and could not be shaved;

she mourned for one year, supporting herself on my grandfather's walking stick. Nobody was allowed to greet her. Since she was the eldest, she was now supposed to get an inheritor (*jater*). She looked for somebody who was old like her. He slept at my grandmother's house and hung his coat on the wall. So I asked her whose coat was that; then she told me that it belonged to my grandfather. He slept for three days, and the fourth day, my grandmother took him to his house, cooked for him and came back. After that he no longer stayed with them.

DIXON: Madam, there is something called *chira* (curse) that we must pay attention to. Sometimes you might refuse to be inherited and go with any man outside secretly, but when you come back home, your child falls sick and dies. The proper protocol for inheritance is whereby a man (*jater*) comes to your house in the morning, you make him some tea and after that, he will take you to his place to introduce you to his wife. If the wife agrees, a dry fish is prepared and herbs will be spread all over the fish, and you eat together.

PHYLLIS: However, there are other cases, which cause problems, for instance, my sister-in-law lost her husband and she was left with three children. She refused to be inherited. So when the children grew up, the first son got married but he was marrying and the wives kept leaving him, so people started telling him that his mother was the one who was chasing them, because she was not inherited. So they went and brought an inheritor for their mother, and the son met a wife who stayed.

AWINO: So you say that a young woman was inherited for the purpose of procreating and for an older woman only a coat was hung to ensure that he [the inheritor] would be available to sit in meetings. When I look at this mama here, she is very senior – she has been in this home for a long time; why can she not conduct the affairs of her own home, since Luos recognised her as *pim*?

MBUSA: *Pim* is not given respect. She is cut out of the equation, because she is old and has reached menopause. She is now like a man. A man cannot be with her sexually. If one does that, it is almost like you are sleeping with a fellow man and as Joluo we do not accept that. She is not respected. She is someone who has been cut off, so it is only her grandchildren that can be close to her.

AWINO: Explain the two to me: she is cut off and yet you also equate her to being like a man, who as you point out has power.

DIXON: Yes, if she had power, she would do these things on her own – build a house, negotiate for dowry, welcome important relatives into the home, amongst others – on her own, but since she doesn't, a man – *dume* [bull] – must be present to help her.

BOYA: A woman is a woman whether she is young or old. She is a woman; she cannot take up any responsibilities in that home.

There are two main issues of interest from this excerpt. The first concerns how a woman's legitimacy and, in turn, a man's power, is asserted in the home (public domain) and enforced by the family (private sphere) upon death. The second is the role of symbols in enforcing this legitimacy. *Ter* becomes a formal institution through which the vacuum of male power due to the death is re-affirmed. A widow agreeing to inheritance, and therefore to a *jater*, positions a *jater* as de facto head of the family who is subsequently charged with decision-making power. Widow inheritance becomes the basis to legitimise a woman's continued presence in the home. However, other symbols emerge in the process of widow inheritance to circumvent physical presence and/or sexual consummation as the only way to assert male authority. For example, the placement of a coat, as an indicator of a man's presence is viewed as a method of power transition between men (late husband and *jater*). The symbolic transition of 'ownership' through the coat serves as a reference point for older women who, while they were not required to live with a man, still required his presence to act as the 'head of the household'. Through the symbolic device of the coat, the surveillance of older women continues as they are bound through a symbolic figurehead to continued performance of the role of a wife and 'proper widow'.

Age matters for a woman's ability to subvert sexual expectations associated with widow inheritance rites. The previous discussion highlights the daily discursive reinterpretation of culture and power. The male participants noted that the respect accorded to a *pim* was not due to her knowledge and/or long-standing association with her marital home; rather it was because her reproductive role had ceased. *Obedo kaka dichwo* – 'she has become like a man'. Yet, despite 'becoming like a man', she was seen as unable to perform designated men's roles in her own home. In their view, the respect for *pim* did not translate into decision-making power. Dixon re-emphasised that the presence and roles of a man in the home were non-negotiable.

The second symbolic and discursive device is *chira*. Very much like the coat, it is discursively deployed to instil fear via the vector of disease and death. The meaning of *chira* in the literature on widow inheritance remains vague at best. It was originally a mysterious illness that was inflicted on an individual who did not adhere to defined and codified cultural practices, such as widow inheritance. However, with the arrival of HIV/AIDS, *chira* began to be used as a euphemism for AIDS. Cultural custodians argued that those who contracted AIDS had failed to follow cultural dictates; *chira* thus became a symbol for a curse. As a result, it is argued that the slow uptake of HIV/AIDS interventions in the Nyanza region was influenced by these definitions and that many individuals thus sought a cultural response to HIV/

AIDS-related illnesses, including sexual cleansing rituals also associated with widowhood rites (NASCOP & MOH, 1998).

Chira is primarily used to negotiate gendered authority through the surveillance of women's bodies and therefore their sexualities. The result is the management of what are considered 'wayward femininities' through the fear of disease caused by women's transgressions. The shifting and perhaps liberal use of *chira* as a symbolic border guard is seen through references to the implicit 'harm' brought about by a refusal to be inherited. The link between *chira* as disease and *chira* as the myth of harm is a key symbolic device used to develop a dialectical association of death, illness and bad luck with a failure to adhere to and obey established cultural norms. In return it becomes the way through which control is exercised through the discursive construction of 'promiscuous and uncontrollable' women. The use of symbols and taboos to circumscribe gendered terrains of power reveals an environment in which femininities and masculinities are contested. These contestations are primarily associated with a vacuum in male power. The discursive reconstruction of a man's power by women through symbolic and essentialised interpretations of roles such as the 'unofficial' man who 'helps' construct a house destabilises the perception of women's power as resting only within the private zone, and instead crosses into the public sphere when women negotiate the terms on which 'new' men enter their lives.

Wayward femininities

The disruption of hitherto identified fixed gendered spaces named as public and private is evident when women exercise constrained choice in even when they accept widow inheritance. One of the primary ways in which power shifts is through women's performances of appropriate responsibilities as 'new widows' by agreeing to be inherited. 'Respectable femininities' remain intact while they subvert commonly held notions of how femininity ought to be performed through the seduction of a potential inheritor. While the literature (see Ogutu, 1995, 2001; Potash, 1978, 1986) points to the fact that designation and agreement about who should inherit the widow rests with the elders and the in-laws, the practice suggests otherwise as illustrated below.

JERUSHA: When your husband dies, you are the one who goes to seduce a man; no one does it for you.

TERESA: Yes, because you are expected to go around pleading with a man to be with you and often it is somebody else's husband. So when he comes, you treat him nicely.

PLISTER: In today's inheritance, you can bring even someone from a different tribe to inherit you. You might be working with a Kikuyu man, and when your husband dies, you can decide to bring him home to build a home for you, and then go back to where you work.

ODONGO: As a young man, I develop an interest in looking for a partner and especially older woman who are easier and cheaper to seduce than a young woman. I can also do a hit and run and then run off to another place. I also think wealth is a big factor. Let me give you an example. If you come with a vehicle, approach me as a peasant and take me somewhere for a drink, I will accept.

OGOLLA: That is not inheritance; that is purely sex. You have not followed Luo culture. A woman cannot direct you to inherit her if you have not cleansed her in the house.

BELDINA: Let us take note of what the lady said that it would be good to forget about sex after your husband's death. If you get inherited, this man will come up with his own rules that you are not used to and that will always lead to some misunderstanding in your marriage. You may find it difficult to adapt and decide to chase him away. If you chase him away those are the cases you hear about men burning houses. There is little you can do, because that is also their land. The children may also get angry and bring chaos in the family. If you get pregnant with this man, they might not be happy. That's why today's inheritance is not good. Women have no voice in the home.

ESTHER: I wanted to clarify from the lady who said that widows do not have a voice in the home. In my opinion, widows have a voice because you are a custodian of that property on behalf of your children or you contributed to creating that wealth with your husband.

PLISTER: Widows have a voice because nothing can go on in the home without your approval. Where women lose their voice is when they begin behaving badly, when their children see them with their new husband in ways in which they did not see their father (cuddling), offering this person food that their father never had, so they begin to lose respect for their mother.

ERNEST: I want to go back to the subject of young men inheriting women. Women are a mess especially when their husbands left some wealth; they will now use this money to buy the boys by buying them clothes.

ONYANGO: Let me give an example: Wambui Otieno[4] and Mbugua. This young man went there for Wambui's wealth. We blame the women for going for those young men, because they are the ones that choose for themselves.

Women are constructed as protagonists who approach and seduce the potential *jater*. This discourse points to a shift and rupture of the terms of wifehood, with the expectation that their roles would only be visible in the private realm. This position is in stark contrast to renewed expectations of them as 'new wives' upon inheritance that requires them to revert to a 'subjugated' position. Interestingly, the focus group interlocutors perceive no tensions (nor are any questions raised) about the new role women are required to play as 'good widows/women' alongside being sexual protagonists in a context where they were previously considered passive actors. The encounters that lead to the identification and pursuit of an inheritor show the power that is held by the widow as an active agent who makes decisions regarding the presence or absence of the man in her life, based on the terms negotiated upon his arrival, as suggested by Plister above.

Nonetheless, the power described above is an uneasy one. It carries with it concerns amongst women about impropriety, which is derived from the communal 'denial' of women as sexual beings, except in designated spaces (marriage). The discomfort and subsequent reconstruction of the power that comes with choice when exercised by women is seen through the reconstruction of a 'widowed single' woman as a prostitute. This idea is developed during a focus group with men discussed next. The subversion of women's power through the construction of their femininities as 'out of control' forms the overarching lens in the following discussion.

In the previous excerpt, Ogolla (overtly) and Ernest (covertly) reject the power exercised by women through their choice of an inheritor. In placing women's choice in the terrain of the 'culturally inappropriate', Ogolla constructs the widows' actions as counter-hegemonic, going against culturally prescribed norms. When women are described as 'out of control and easy', it is based on two correlations. The first is that women with financial resources can no longer be controlled and that women who have been married before or are older are less demanding in terms of their expectations around seduction. In both instances, women with access to financial resources and older women are easy targets for younger men who have contributed to commercialising widow inheritance.

Widows' re-appropriation of cultural norms, even though rejected by men, does not have a cultural basis, particularly when the very sites within which rites should be performed are used and not dismissed. When Ogolla locates the house as the site, which determines that 'inheritance' has officially occurred, he gives power back to the woman. As indicated previously, the household is the space where women negotiate and hold power. A woman exercising power in public by identifying a suitor and concluding the 'contract' in private points to layers of transgression across gendered sites of power. These debates cannot be viewed as separate from an ongoing struggle with redefinitions of dominant masculinities.

Younger men are constructed as victims, by rehashing the story of Wambui and Mbugua to illustrate the growing empirical evidence to support the claim that older widows coerce younger and unemployed men into relationships. A distinction is made between the role of sex in inheritance and sex for pleasure. Women with economic power are discursively developed as lacking control, noting that they misappropriate property by being with younger men. Younger men are not viewed as opportunistic or predatory. Women's sexual autonomy is contested.

ONYANGO: It is true that, when a woman loses her husband, she is the one to seduce the man. So maybe after some months, she will chase away the man and bring in another man. I am an inheritor and the big problem is the question of respect. So men burn the houses, so that we see where she will live with that new man.

ADUDA: What happens with a lot of young women today is that they already had an in-law whom they liked before the man died. A woman who has been inherited is a woman who has already lived with a man and she has experience in marriage, so it's so difficult to handle her, unlike a newly married woman. Nowadays, married woman have really changed: they always behave like young girls in that even when you call her the name 'mother', she doesn't like it – they lack respect.

ERNEST: On that matter, the reason why women say the inheritors are bad is often because the men want to control them, because you might see that a woman is misusing the property of her late husband to buy luxurious things, and if you try to ask her, it starts a quarrel. What causes the burning of houses is this: the inheritor spends too much time where he has been 'seconded', and abandons his primary home. His wife could potentially send him away and when he returns to this other home, he is chased away. Meanwhile, he is the very person who 'built' the house, meaning that he stood as the man of the home and cleanses her, after which her behaviour changes.

ONYANGO: I will speak about what I have seen. A long time ago, when women were inherited, they gave birth with their inheritors. Today, all the women who are inherited are older, and even the young ones do not have children with their inheritors. These women are just inherited for fun. The respect that women who were inherited had for their inheritors is non-existent today. The respect she gave her husband, she does not give the inheritor, so you cannot control her. Women who are older and inherited have no respect and cannot be controlled. Today, inheritance does not help at all, because women are not giving birth. There is also no development you can take to that home. The inheritor often goes to exploit not to develop.

The changing forms of masculinity emerge through the narrative of an inheritor, Onyango, who increasingly feels that his roles, particularly those aspects associated with the assertion of control over a woman, are usurped. They (inheritors) find themselves in the position of an invited guest in a home where they are unable to exert much power. The idea of women in control, in a terrain that has traditionally had the man as the 'aggressor' and protagonist, is unsettling. 'Out of control' women make unilateral decisions regarding the use of resources, exercise bodily autonomy and do not defer to men in heterosexual relationships. In this instance, the source of power – economic resources – seems to have shifted the scales unfavourably. 'Choice' effectively disrupts the narratives of continuity and purity, particularly if, as constructed above, choices are equally exercised around their sexual partners. The 'new widows' are constructed as being unable to 'control' themselves due to their pursuit of intimacy and pleasure, instead of celibacy or reproduction with a designated inheritor.

Respectable femininities and reproduction

Children are positioned as powerful interlocutors in their mother's life due to their link to the home through ancestral land/inheritance. The performances of 'respectable femininities' are situated within the framework of continuity. Continuity here is connected to the lineage, but is also strongly linked to respectability. The articulation of a good mother and wife and the potential for deviation within a new union is constructed as problematic. Consequently, desexualising women or performing chastity becomes essential to managing 'badly behaved' women. Reproduction becomes a major zone that discursively constructs and defines women's sexualities, as well as shaping them as legitimate actors within the home, because they define and propagate the 'nation'. The focus on women as reproducers of nations is informed by the political debates in Kenya at the time of my research, which heightened a focus on the 'nation's' survival. The resurgence of the importance of childbirth, continuity, purity and a 'national' legacy was a key thread.

ADUDA [MAN PARTICIPANT]: Your brother might die and the woman he leaves behind is still young, so the woman should be inherited so that she could give birth to a child who can be named after him.
BETTY [WOMAN PARTICIPANT]: So the Luos brought that issue [widow inheritance] to get another man for the girl so that she could give birth and the children can be recognised as the late husband's children. So I support it in terms of continuing that lineage.

PHYLLIS: [WOMAN PARTICIPANT]: I agree that it is a good practice to ensure that you get someone to stay with you and give children to that home – so that she can raise the flag of that home and preserve the name of the man.

DIXON: [MAN PARTICIPANT]: One of the reasons the Luo also insisted that young widows like you were inherited was to ensure that there is clarity on who you are now with and that the children born after that will become the late husband's children. One of the major things that made the Luo inherit is to bring continuity by ensuring that more children are born.

SELINE [WOMAN PARTICIPANT]: A woman was inherited so that she could have children and the name of the late husband is established, so that a minister or president can emerge.

NGOYE: This is why any clever woman will identify the man to the children – that he is their father and will be handling issues in that home. When the husband dies, the elders could sit down and decide who will inherit the woman.

DIXON: In our history as *JoLuo*, women who are inherited and have children from those unions are different. This is because women who are inherited have a lot of love and when you sleep with her, the child will be extremely intelligent and lucky. One such example was Jaramogi Odinga. We have many examples in the village where your own children refuse to go to school, but where you have had children through inheritance, the children excel. The inherited wives were disciplined and had no quarrels, especially in bed.

Young women propagating the nation during moments of crisis became a key argument for the value of widow inheritance. Young women became key to producing children to maintain the family lineage on the one hand and ensuring the community's continuity on the other. Women's reproductive capacities became framed as 'communal responsibility' and are predicated on some form of 'purity'. The insistence through widow inheritance rites for an appointed *jater* serves as a surveillance mechanism to facilitate an acceptable lineage. The construction of the 'good' inherited widow who exudes love and discipline in sufficient measure to contribute effectively to the birth of 'important' children emerges above as a counter-narrative to the 'bad' widow who needs to be contained. The 'good widow' is constructed here as one who conducts her affairs with the full approval of the clan members, thus earning herself dignity and respect. Currency is subsequently placed on the women, and therefore on the children born out of inheritance unions, through reference to political leadership. The identification of a historical political figure in Kenyan and Luo politics as a product of an inheritance union discursively reinforces the link between widowhood rites, preservation of the nation and access to state resources via leadership.

Widow inheritance and gender identity 55

The sexualisation of a widow in terms that do not challenge normative perceptions of womanhood, motherhood and femininity is seen through the immediate construction of a man's presence as an inheritor, thus creating an opportunity to 'rescue' the woman's honour through widow inheritance and marriage as legitimising narratives. The power of women in reconfiguring national dynamics and therefore legitimising their citizenship in the Luo nation is predicated on being 'good', where 'good' women from the previous analysis are those who love and do not quarrel – in essence, women who are 'controllable'.

Conclusion

This chapter set out to explore the ways in which gendered identities are discursively re-constructed. Examining discourses produced around widow inheritance rites reveals a complex process of negotiating identities through a continuous re-inscription of 'conservative' gender norms. While the fluidity and varying performances of gender occur daily, the contestations in this instance are occasioned by an event (death) and a transitional process (widowhood) that create the space for the disruption of a normative gendered order. The fear of this disruption raises three key issues. The first is the way in which power is circumscribed and controlled to arrogate power to men. Through a network of spaces (public and private), symbols (coats), roles, responsibilities and taboos (*chira*), mechanisms are created to assert both actual and symbolic male power and widowhood rites, and primarily the need for a *jater* becomes the vehicle to reassert these norms. However, the process of re-inscribing norms is not a linear one. It is accompanied by the production of counter-narratives and counter-hegemonic narratives, and this is the second issue.

Counter-hegemonic narratives are acts of subversion deployed by women who challenge, usurp and subvert the devices deployed to maintain male hegemonic power. This is seen in the symbolic deployment of male power through alternative routes to inheritance or, as seen in the latter section of this chapter, through choices made over reproduction. However, these approaches are mediated by counter-narratives developed by men who reconstruct women's acts of subversion through the vectors of dirt and pollution – prostitution and promiscuity. These counter-narratives produced by men point to destabilised and re-constructed masculinities.

The third issue is the redefinition of gender and sexuality, which, while important to local order and control, also filter through to the national sphere. The visibility of this community's[5] struggle with changing configurations of gendered relationships and accompanying expectations is seen in how both visible and invisible boundaries are reconfigured. Women emerge

56 Widow inheritance and gender identity

as boundary markers, due to their key role as reproducers of nations, which results in the surveillance not only of their bodies, but also of their physical movement: this is done by keeping them in the home through the act of inheritance or challenging their sexual choices with partners other than those sanctioned by the clan. The next chapter will focus on the linkage between widow inheritance and nation-/state-building by examining the role of language and boundary creation in consolidating a nation within the state project.

Notes

1 Interviews conducted with 20 widows as part of the pilot phase of the field research. While they do not form part of the data under analysis, they challenge the notion of male power in useful ways.
2 I develop the discussion on boundaries in the next chapter.
3 This was evident in the jeering and interjections that surrounded this utterance.
4 Wambui Otieno was a well-known Kenyan Mau Mau freedom fighter, a woman of many firsts. In 1985, she challenged the patrilineal rights to the husband's body (S.M. Otieno) upon his death, which resulted in a court case that has drawn significant popular and theoretical analysis. Her 2003 marriage at 67 to a 28-year-old man sparked major debates in the country.
5 This community is represented here through the few, yet important, 60 voices that I engaged with during my field work.

4 Discursive boundaries
Building nations

The destabilisation created by death and the transitional nature of widowhood provides fodder for the rehearsal of 'respectable' femininities and 'powerful' masculinities. These discursive constructions are responses to counter-hegemonic narratives and strategies deployed by women to challenge hegemonic discourses that privilege and arrogate power to men. The link between the local (home, clan) and the national (state, country) spheres emerges through discourses on continuity and reproduction as mechanisms to insist on a 'pure nation'. The counter-narratives developed by male participants construct two kinds of women (widows) – 'good' and 'bad'. These discussions etch both invisible and visible boundaries, specifically as they pertain to physical movement and choices. The second reason is connected to boundaries as a means of understanding transition and transformation and draws on the theoretical framework developed in Chapter 1, which recognises that women may be controlled in the interests of demarcating and preserving the identities of national/ethnic groups (see Kandiyoti, 1991). Regulations concerning whom a woman may marry, and what the legal status of her offspring is, aim at reproducing the boundaries of the symbolic identity of a group (Yuval-Davis & Anthias, 1989; Douglas, 2002).

Constructing boundaries and defining borders

Discursive patterns used to create and define individual boundaries and communal borders emerge during discussions on the history and function of widow inheritance, as well as from participants' reflections on the practicalities of the process in terms of who could inherit and why. I distinguish between two discursive approaches to the creation of borders. The first develops ideas around the function of the 'insider' (*jater*) and historicises this role as a means of creating an internal border. The second constructs and 'rejects' the 'outsider' through a local and national discourse justifying

58 *Discursive boundaries*

this 'rejection'. The role of myth and history, as well as the codification of Luo traditions and norms as mechanisms to affirm these two tropes, is also explored.

The 'insider'

AWINO: Why was widow inheritance practised amongst the Luo?

AMOS [MAN PARTICIPANT]: Inheritance was started a long time ago when the Luo came from Sudan to Kenya. People [men] would die along the way and a woman would be given to her in-law to continue the journey with him, to take her (*tere*) to the final destination.

JULIUS [MAN PARTICIPANT]: On widow inheritance, we are not the ones that started it, but we found it. Your brother might die, and the woman he leaves behind is still young. So the woman was inherited so that she could give birth to a child who could be named after him. This had to be an in-law in the home and not an outsider.

LILLIAN [WOMAN PARTICIPANT]: Amongst the Luo, when one wants to marry, they look at the background of the person: where she comes from; her people. So when the husband dies, they look for somebody who can take care of her so that she won't bring up a child who does not belong to the community. So it was necessary to bring somebody with the same blood as the late husband.

ERNEST [MAN PARTICIPANT]: A long time ago, a woman would be inherited by the husband's brother, and the elders would then advise the in-law to go and continue the brother's name.

MBUSA [WOMAN PARTICIPANT]: As a parent, I would like my daughter to marry a Luo man who knows the culture.

The explanations above reveal different routes to naming the importance of the 'insider', used here to refer to the brother[1] of the dead husband. However, they also point to similarities in the overarching explanatory framework. Three approaches emerge: the first is located in history; the second is linked to family and continuity; while the third moves from the family to the larger Luo nation. The first route to explaining the importance of the 'insider' asserts this preference as time tested and based on the migratory patterns of the Luo people. It invokes the idea of care and compassion through the ideas of 'accompaniment' and 'taking care of your brother's own'. In locating the 'insider' narrative in written history, Amos bases it on a widely recognised 'true' record of a people's norms, thus initiating a discourse of continuity. He develops the idea that the practice is unchangeable due to its roots in over two centuries of praxis, and thus begins to draw invisible boundaries. These boundaries define responsibilities for men in the community and concomitantly frame a widow's conduct upon the death of her husband. The discourse of continuity is also suggested – albeit in veiled terms – through the metaphor of 'completing journeys'. This is seen through the importance of 'appointing' a brother to take the widow to the 'final destination'.

The place of history and continuity is built on by Julius in his assertion that widow inheritance is a found practice. This is the second discursive strand but it is developed further by deploying reproduction as an important part of that continuity. Participants Amos, Lillian and Ernest introduce purity as a critical aspect of reproduction. This is seen in the discussions around the negotiation of marriage bonds, the knowledge of one's history, linkages to the lineage of the dead husband and, finally, the importance of tribe. The third discursive strand justifies the importance of the 'insider' by adopting 'culture' as a trope, and reflects a move from the local (family) to the nation (Luo). By introducing the 'outsider', participants Julius and Lillian begin to move the debate from the local. They introduce a larger boundary, which defines the (Luo) nation through its cultural norms and that therefore requires continuity to ascertain cohesion. Douglas (2002: 172) notes that, whenever lines of security are precarious, such as those that offer the potential to collapse identity narratives, discourses about pollution come to the support of those claiming their own identities against 'others'. Douglas notes, too, that ideas about sexual pollution are also more developed in areas where clan exogamy is the practice. The wife is viewed as a competitor and a threat. The exogamous nature of Luo marriage cannot be underestimated as a driving factor here, as a woman is always an outsider and, as such, efforts to 'keep' her are grounded in the ever-present potential of her leaving.[2] In all routes to framing the 'insider' and affirming invisible boundaries, women are portrayed as participants in a process that is produced through history, the clan and the elders as custodians of knowledge. The role of a wife is situated within obedience and acceptance of found practices. The centrality of wives to purity is affirmed, but has to be enforced through various roles and narratives that centralise men as key decision makers. The discursive production of the 'outsider' cannot be examined in isolation from the 'insider'.

The 'outsider' – *Jamwa*

NGOYA [MAN PARTICIPANT]: If my daughter brings home maybe a Luhya and tells me she wants to marry him, I will remind her of Luo culture that condemns intermarrying with other tribes. That's why the term '*jamwa*' still exists, which is a person who will bring bad behaviour. If she marries a Luhya, she will end up destroying the lineage of the Luo; she will just marry him, but will not have my blessing.

JANE [WOMAN PARTICIPANT]: The reason why the Luo did not want any other tribe was because you might get a killer and then you give birth to somebody who will also be killing people in the area. So it was better for them to get at least somebody with the same blood.

HERBERT [MAN PARTICIPANT]: There are different tribes. If you get married to, for example, a Kikuyu, you can have children. When the children grow up, the woman might decide to take them and go back to her home, leaving you with nothing. So it will force you to start a new life, and that's why the Luo prefer to marry their own who understand that the children born are the property of that home and community. Tribalism will always continue.

MBUSA [MAN PARTICIPANT]: Our children marry other tribes, our children like marrying other women from various tribes, but you will not find men from different tribes marrying our daughters; that is why our culture is ruined, because this woman does not know and will not follow Luo culture. When our child dies, the woman will take away the children and go with them.

The production of the 'outsider' discourse, as seen above, hinges on continuity as a major thread. Conventions of reproduction and 'culture' are the main ways in which aversion to a non-Luo is articulated. The role of children in building and consolidating the nation also arose through diverse issues: the potential loss of their (Luo) children upon the death of a husband, the lack of knowledge of 'culture' that would contribute to the widow's departure or the inability to control the gene pool through references to the kind of children to which one could potentially give birth. Finally, there was the dual concern that, on the one hand, 'blamed' young Luo men for marrying outside the tribe, but also implied that the decision not to marry outside the tribe was also being exercised by other ethnic groups in their choice not to marry Luo women. The potential loss of children and the lack of 'cultural' knowledge are interlinked, and are presented as an assertion of patriarchy and patriliny in asserting ownership over children and wives. The fact that this authority cannot be enforced on a woman who does not identify with the 'tribe's laws' is problematic. Aversion to the 'outsider' woman is thus enforced by a control and surveillance discourse rooted in patriarchy and patriliny. The inability to control the gene pool through the introduction of a *jamwa* (foreigner) who cannot be trusted, as well as the description of children born from mixed unions, begins to give rise to a different narrative, one based on the notion of 'purity'.

The purity discourse is legitimised in two main ways. The first way is by arguing that 'Luo culture' condemned marriage to 'outsiders'. Through unwritten law that affirms the 'insider', emphasis is placed on time and the 'authenticity' that comes with such continuity. In removing authority from the individual and placing it elsewhere (i.e. in Luo culture), the participants suggest a site of power, but one that cannot be challenged, owing to its lack of tangibility in the form of an institution or person. The second way in which the purity discourse is legitimised is by introducing the possibility that this is an approach pursued by other ethnic groups. In reference to the disparity between Luo men marrying 'other' women and Luo women marrying into other ethnic groups, Mbusa alludes to the possibility that other ethnic groups also recognise the importance of 'purity' and that this is not simply a Luo attitude.

The 'outsider' discourse progresses through a connection to the nation/state. Drawing on myth, personal narratives and historical cases, the participants below begin to develop an empirical base on which to ground a visible communal boundary.

HERBERT [MAN PARTICIPANT]: Most of tribes, even when we marry [into them], we can't know their secrets. You can live with a woman for over ten years and not know many things about her, so that's why we find that our bright Luo people get lost when they marry these other tribes. You find that you might marry a Kikuyu and when you divorce, she will go away with all your children. You will always be scared and when people tell stories, they do not want you to listen, because they believe that you will take it back to the Luo land. You all remember the story of Luanda Magere.[3]

SELLINE [WOMAN PARTICIPANT]: Look at the story of *S.M. Otieno*: when he died, the Luo wanted his body to be buried in Siaya, but Wambui wanted his body. But the Luo took him and buried him. So the Luo believe in bones and flesh and they believe that when a man dies, he should be buried at his home.[4]

INGRID [WOMAN PARTICIPANT]: We have a Kikuyu man who lives in Kisumu. He came here as a fisherman, so he had a Luo wife at the port. Even during the post-election period, she protected him, but they always had domestic problems. The local villagers began threatening him, telling him that he would be chased away after he had finished constructing the house. So one night that man wanted some money to buy some cigarettes. She asked where he was going to get cigarettes at that hour of the night. He told her that if she didn't give him the money, he would kill her. They started fighting and the man took a rope and tied this woman up. He took a knife and when he was about to stab her, the knife fell. The woman ran out and hid, but did not cry for help. The man took the two children and went away with them. When she came back to the house, she could not find the kids. She started screaming for help. They searched for the kids and eventually found them in the morning dumped near a bush by the lake. So bringing somebody like a Kikuyu into Luo society is still so difficult, particularly if he can kill children that are not his. The man escaped and was never found. It is not easy.

CAROLINE [WOMAN PARTICIPANT]: If, for example, my son comes home with a Kikuyu lady, I won't accept her, because she is not my tribe and I don't know about her background, but if it's a Luo, I can agree. If I relate this to what happened during the post-election violence, I don't think it could be easy with any other tribe, because what brought all the problems has not been solved. So that bitterness will not end, especially in the state that Kenya is in now.

DIXON [MAN PARTICIPANT]: Politically it is worse, because you might be a leader and marry somebody from a different tribe and you can easily be killed by your wife. [He is referring to rumours that circulated about a murder attempt on a prominent Luo politician by his Meru wife in the aftermath of the post-election crisis.] We want unity within tribes, but we must distinguish between political *hera* (love) and culture. I suggest that our Luo leaders should sit down and discuss that, if it is a must we intermarry, they should specify the tribes to intermarry with, e.g. Luhya, Kisii but not Kikuyu, Kamba, Meru, Embu.

Each participant develops the 'outsider' narrative from different trajectories. Myth and past and current history are offered as 'evidence' of the importance of visible boundaries that can be ascertained by maintaining a pure lineage. The first participant offers mythology as a basis for comprehending why visible boundaries must be maintained by avoiding marriage to 'outsiders'. He also introduces the notion of children's intelligence, the general superior ability to underscore the greater loss to the Luo nation, not only in terms of the men who marry 'outside', but also in terms of their progeny. He builds on a previous narrative through the notion of secrecy, thus developing the thread that a concomitant process of 'locking out' 'outsiders' occurs amongst other ethnic groups too. The subsequent evocation of historical cases grounds the perceived incompatibility between ethnic groups. Selline, who recalls the *S.M. Otieno* case, turns a family (clan) struggle into a national struggle by mentioning that 'the Luo wanted his body to be buried in Siaya'. The immediate homogenisation and creation of 'us' versus 'them' moves the 'outsider' question from the family to the nation (Luo). The need to protect the Luo nation can be read in the valorisation of norms, the value attached to burial and bodies and the elaborate rituals surrounding both marriage and death.

The third and fourth participants situate the 'outsider' discourse in struggle, which inadvertently locates national (Luo) purity in a statist discourse. In recalling events surrounding a political crisis, both Ingrid and Caroline refer to local choices having national (Kenyan) repercussions. They situate mistrust and allude to deliberate killings – 'if he can kill children that are not his' – as a basis for irrevocable visible (ethnic) boundaries. Previously 'invisible', 'internal' decisions around marriage that are often negotiated through cultural norms and practices such as widow inheritance are now anchored within larger state contestations that justify 'visible' boundaries.

Dixon firmly locates the question of Luo 'purity' within the social, political and economic contestations in Kenya in 2008. Rumour was a mechanism that was widely used during the post-election period to spread fear and heighten tensions about the risks amongst various ethnic groups, particularly where interethnic betrayal was concerned, as one participant refers to in the previous excerpt. His reference was not simply about rehashing the discursive 'outsider' who cannot be trusted, as has been done by other participants. He speaks to the 'political threats' that such unions can cause. In identifying specific ethnic groups, Dixon urges 'permanent' ways to resolve what he sees as a problem of 'contagion' through intermarriage. By using the word 'must', he hints at his discomfort with the idea of intermarriage, but also indicates his willingness to defer to political authority, should such intermarriage be deemed politically expedient. He is more explicit in his reference to 'preferable' and 'non-preferable' ethnic groups, making a direct link to ethnic divisions in the country. It is important to point out that the counter-discourse that emerged was a public and heightened need to show that interethnic unions worked and that they would, in effect, contribute to ethnic dialogue and cohesion. This narrative was used to counter both rumours and stories carried in the media that pointed to familial divisions because of political differences. The mobilisation of ethnicity as political tool in Kenya entrenched both visible and invisible boundaries in ways that are gendered. The political crisis in 2008 elevated the gendered nature of these debates, moving them into the political sphere and therefore making them visible.

'Political expediency' as a mechanism for defining 'visible' boundaries is picked up through a distinction between political tolerance (*hera*) and 'culture'. Political love/tolerance is informed by the need to co-exist due to the geographical 'accident' of being in one country. 'Culture', on the other hand, is an absolute that needs to be preserved and should remain 'uncontaminated', irrespective of political expediency. These views draw clear boundaries between the 'insider' and 'outsider'. The relevance of this distinction to the national (Kenyan) political process is in entrenching widow inheritance as a 'quality control' mechanism. Ethnic differences mobilised by a contested presidential election in 2007 resulted in politically constructed alliances between ethnic groups, based on the constellations of power at the state level. This was reflected in daily discussions amongst Kenyans regarding who were allies and who were not, and who could and could not be trusted, but also how ethnic alliances would serve as a political solution to an electoral crisis. The coalition government's creation of the Commission for National Cohesion was an attempt to respond to this fracture in the social fabric.

Conclusion

Widow inheritance becomes the vehicle through which individual (homestead) boundaries are defined. However, the discursive development sees the importance of the practice embedded in history, thereby beginning to assert permanence and its relevance to the sustainability of a nation (the Luo). To indicate the potential threat to this sustainability, the discourse shifts from the personal (individual homestead) to one that implicates a nation (the Luo community in general). This progression allows for the assertion of urgency and larger losses, particularly when strong co-relations are made to the contestations at the state level. Context and a political moment therefore serve as a trigger for reasserting the value of widow inheritance as a mechanism for consolidating numbers and ensuring national cohesion.

The 'insider' and 'outsider' boundaries are developed through the construction of 'pure nations' with the resolution of emerging tensions nestled in the surveillance of women's bodies and their sexualities. Surveillance becomes a mechanism to 'order' the community through narratives of purity, coherence and continuity. Widow inheritance thus serves as a 'quality control' mechanism that ensures the production of 'good' women who recognise the need for communal control of their reproductive choices. This is seen through discourses that single out the importance of childbearing with the 'right' man – i.e. the 'insider'. This control results in stricter surveillance of Luo women, and it is accompanied by the construction of a boundary around 'other' women marrying into the tribe. This surveillance of sexuality reifies both the reproductive and marital space and situates power in the hands of women. However, this power is countered through the construction of roles, responsibilities, myths and taboos that reassert men's power through the clan and *jater*. This is primarily due to the construction of non-hegemonic masculinities represented by *joter* as powerless.

Notes

1 The term 'brother' is used broadly, and is not restricted to the nuclear family, but extends to cousins or any other male members of the same clan.

Discursive boundaries 65

2 See Chapter 3 for a discussion by Ogutu (2001) of 'becoming' a Luo wife.
3 Luanda Magere is the story of a Luo hero who married a Nandi woman who betrayed him by revealing to his tribe where his power lay, which was in his shadow and not his body (see Okoth, 2006). The story of Luanda Magere was remade into a Broadway-style musical by a popular Kenyan musician as part of citizens' efforts towards reconciliation during the 2007/08 election-triggered violence (see Teng'o, 2003).
4 The discursive production of the distinction between house and home is credited to the *S.M. Otieno* case (see Cohen & Odhiambo, 1992). The 'home' is the rural and ancestral base where all rituals, including those related to death, must be concluded. The urban abode, in contrast, is considered a 'house' – a temporary transitional space occasioned by the need to work and live away from the ancestral land.

5 Gendered language and culture

A book interested in discourse must centre the role of gendered language in the production of culture. Language has been described as the primary means through which we maintain or contest old meanings and construct or resist new ones (see Cameron, 1998, 2001; Eckert & McGonnell-Ginet, 2003). The importance of language, particularly its performativity and its embodiment, is based on feminist epistemologies that recognise its role in constructing and shaping masculinities and femininities (see Cameron, 1998; Lakoff, 1975; Miller & Swift, 1976; Spender, 1980). A long history of Northern feminist epistemologies has pointed to the intersection between gender and language. Scholars such as Lakoff (1975), Miller and Swift (1976) and Spender (1980) have all published studies that suggest the existence of a feminine way of using language. Lakoff (1975) argues that women have a different way of speaking from men that reflects and produces a subordinate position in society. This language, she argues, renders women's speech tentative, powerless and trivial, thereby disqualifying them from positions of power and authority (Lakoff, 1975: 112). Thorne et al. (1983) argue that an examination of differences – such as the contexts, who was talking to whom, for what purposes and in what kind of setting – would yield more illuminating insights about gender, power and language use (Thorne et al., 1983: 12). I take seriously Scott's (1987) distinction of the 'public' and 'hidden' transcript. Scott (1987: 20) advises that it is necessary to pay close attention to political acts that are disguised as offstage, for this may help to map a realm of dissent.

> Given the usual power of dominant elites to compel performances from others, the discourse of the public transcript is a decidedly lopsided discussion . . . it is a highly partisan and partial narrative. It is designed to be impressive, to affirm and naturalize the power of dominant elites and to conceal or euphemise the dirty linen of their rule.
>
> (Scott, 1987: 18)

The 'hidden transcript', he argues, is the privileged site for non-hegemonic, contrapuntal, dissident, subversive discourse that is often evasive, but critical (Scott, 1987: 25). Scott also signals a third realm that plays out in public view – a partly sanitised, ambiguous and coded version of the 'hidden transcript' that is visible in rumour, gossip, jokes, songs and euphemisms. The performativity and strategic deployment of language through various codes, as Scott (1987) points out, will form an important lens for my analysis. Specifically, I will analyse how gendered linguistic practices and devices create narratives of permanence and continuity around widow inheritance. Secondly, I will examine the role of metaphor in discussions on widow inheritance as a counter-hegemonic gendered linguistic practice.

Gendered linguistic practices[1]

The organisation of verbal interaction during my field work was important in as far as it highlighted how women conveyed their ideas and how their proposals were taken up.

JUDITH: You can't tell why inheritance because we started seeing it a long time ago, so we grew up seeing it happening. So you must be inherited if you have children; you are inherited so that you do not mess up their future [i.e. the potential to inherit property or the processes related to getting married are protected by remarrying in that home] and if you do not have children it helps to continue the lineage. Secondly, when the house gets old and somebody comes to fix it, you are being asked that where is the man in this home, so that he can come and build it, so that's why we got inherited.

PHYLLIS: I agree that it is a good practice to ensure that you get someone to stay with and give children to that home. So that she can raise the flag of that home and preserve the name of the man. However, there are other cases, which cause problems; for instance, my sister-in-law lost her husband, she was left with three children, she refused to be inherited. So when the children grew up, the first son got married, but he was marrying and the wives kept leaving him, so people started telling him that his mother was the one who was chasing them, because she was not inherited. So they went and brought an inheritor for their mother, and the son got a wife who stayed.

LILLIAN: Long time ago, people, women below 40 years were being inherited and those above 50 years were given cigarettes, those who were younger gave birth and the baby is named after the late husband. We were being told that this was a good practice because they used to agree with the wife of the inheritor, women were not forced and they maintained one woman. But today's inheritance somebody can even inherit more than six wives and you might be the eighth woman and not even aware that he already have six of them. This is what led to the increase of HIV and AIDS infection. And there are some men who know that they are sick, but they go and inherit a woman who is not sick. So I don't support today's inheritance, because you can't differentiate between a sick and healthy person.

GERTRUDE [WOMAN PARTICIPANT]: We were three women married to one man. I was the eldest and did not want to be inherited because I was saved [i.e. was a Christian]. I was forced so that I could open ways for my younger co-wives. I was inherited by this man seated here. I did not go to church for six months because I had transgressed and only returned to church afterwards. My in-law is still with me today.

ABILA [WOMAN PARTICIPANT]: My husband died in 1998 and in that home we were two women, so we had to be inherited, because one of the sons had died. We were told that he could not be buried until we were inherited. We were also told that we had to be inherited by one man. So I said I will get my own man and asked the elders to give me one day [to do so]. I went to Ahero and met one of my friends, and told her what had happened. She told me that there was one of her in-laws who wanted a woman, so I told her to call him, then he came and we talked. So we went back and the two of us went with our men, but the first wife wanted to trick me by saying that I should be inherited first because her man had not come. So I told him [i.e. the man she had found] he had to go because, as the younger wife, there was no way I could be inherited before the other one, but being a non-Luo, he did not understand this. He spent the night in my house for three days until the burial, and I later on met this Ugenya man and he inherited me.

JUDITH [WOMAN PARTICIPANT]: You can't tell why inheritance [first came about], because we started seeing it a long time ago, so we grew up with it, so you must be inherited. If you have kids, you are inherited so that you do not mess up their future [i.e. the potential to inherit and get married is protected by remarrying in that home], and if you do not have children, it helps to continue the lineage. Secondly, when the house gets old and somebody comes to fix it, you are asked where the man is in this home so that he can come and build it, so that's why we got inherited.

AKINYI [WOMAN PARTICIPANT]: We were inherited because we were told that we are being protected from death, but we find that with or without inheritance, people still die, so I don't know where this death is coming from.

When women participants explained their understanding of the history and importance of widow inheritance, it was based on personal experience – their own or those of close family members. They made no claim to possessing 'factual' or historical information regarding the roots of the practice. This was reflected in the way in which they articulated their ideas, which positioned them as implementers, not as active agents. Women expressed doubt, not of themselves but of the authenticity of the hegemonic 'explanations' for inheritance. Women participants nonetheless pointed to their continued pursuit of the practice because they were told that it was necessary. This occurred, despite the potential conflict with their beliefs and/or the very norms that are argued to be historically preferred, as can be seen through Abila's narration. This discursive pattern of conflict between implementation and discourse occurred across most of the focus group discussions.

The linguistic patterns deployed by the men participants were different. While the initial discussions may have started with an acknowledgement that this was a 'found' practice, the conversations became progressively rooted in 'fact'. The men, as can be seen in the excerpt below, spoke with each other and built on each other's ideas. In essence, they corroborated a meta-narrative. They did not engage with what the women had to say, and if they did, it was to argue that the view expressed was indicative of the problem of 'now', or to 'help'. Men participants drew from a seemingly unchallengeable base, which was written history based on Luo migratory patterns. The men thus portrayed themselves as authorities on the norms, traditions and 'laws' of the Luo. They pointed to the historicity of the practice, hinting at its unchanging nature due to its resilience over decades. By linking time and the origin of a people to the debate, the men slowly entrenched a discursive practice that stressed continuity and the need for inheritance to be relevant in the here and now due to its role in defining Luo personhood.

MBUSA: Our culture as Luo from Sudan dictated that women were unclean and the in-law came in to cleanse her. Others can add.

GENGA: Inheritance has been maintained in Luo society because, if a man dies, the old men would sit and discuss who among them will inherit the widow, not borrowing somebody from another area. Nowadays, women import men from other areas, people whose backgrounds are not well known, and once you behave like that, the old men would not bother to discuss your issue, because you have gone astray. The young men have taken advantage of this to get support. If we could back to our old customs where people are willing to be guided, that would be very good, because you know the home of the person and your wife knows there is a co-wife; that would be good and very normal.

In legitimising their discourse through a history that was progressively constructed as communal. The men participants began to entrench gender ideologies that framed them as authorities on larger community matters relating to the Luo people. The discursive pattern revealed mutual corroboration amongst the men. They did not deviate from the 'script' that had been set by the first man who spoke. Through this mechanism, they indirectly countered the women participants because they (the men) were drawing from a more authoritative base – written history. The men spoke directly about the women in the space, whether it was in direct reference to tough-minded in-laws in the space who were giving them trouble or drawing examples using women in the space, including me. The discursive practices deployed by men constructed them as custodians of culture, women as participants and the 'protection' of the Luo nation as the greater goal through narratives of continuity and purity deployed through taboo (*chola* and *chira*).

The linguistic devices deployed by women, which reflected uncertainty and willingness to acquiesce to found practices, revealed fluidity in their personal processes and those associated with inheritance. This fluidity was highlighted by pointing to the contradictions between the myths associated with widow inheritance and the reality, as reflected in their personal narratives. The contradictions in the practice emerged through the personal narratives, which were not rooted in fixed historical paradigms, thus suggesting the potential for subversion. By choosing to see the experience of widow inheritance as heterogeneous, the women thus destabilised the notion of homogenised national identities by giving power to the individual.

However, the reasons why people change linguistic norms and how they change them are important in as far these linguistic practices support hetero-normative gender ideologies and norms. The use of the modals, *nego* (should) and *nyaka* (must/ought to), or simple reference to 'this is how it is' (*mae kaka en*), featured prominently in the linguistic patterns of the men interlocutors. These patterns denote expectations of ideal behaviour and personal obligation, which are articulated by those in positions of authority or custodians of power. By using modals, men move away from a personal narrative and embrace a national (Luo) one. Through this process, an obligation is imposed, emphasising the importance of sticking to time-tested methods in comparison to the more tentative present. As can be seen from the following excerpt, the presence of absolutes as ways of conversing about rites related to widow inheritance or gender

Gendered language and culture 71

considerations pointed to the ways in which identities are shaped by gendered linguistic devices. For example, what women can and cannot do and what was and was not allowed can clearly be seen in these explanations of widow inheritance:

AWINO: What was the purpose of widow inheritance amongst the Luo?
AWITI: When your brother dies, the wife becomes unclean (*chola*). So, the widow in Luo culture is dressed in a black dress with a mark on the sleeve of a dress made for her. This is a symbol that this woman has lost her husband. The woman wears this dress in mourning for her husband. The woman can mourn for a year and the mourning officially stops when the elders sit down and discuss [the situation]; they will decide who becomes responsible for their brother's household and his wife. An unclean woman is not allowed to enter the home of anyone else, share meals or greet anyone. According to Luo customs, the man will buy a mat; they would spend the night on the mat; and in the morning, the woman shaves the hair on her head and private parts. After that, the widow is now free.
AMOS: So this inheritance was started a long time ago when the Luo came from Sudan, walking to Kenya. People [men] would die on the way and a woman would be given to her in-law to continue the journey with him, to take her to the final destination (*tere*). So inheritance started long ago and is not bad.
MBUSA: Our culture as Luo from Sudan dictated that women were unclean and the in-law came in to cleanse her. Others can add.

However, the invocation of modals during the focus group discussions cannot be abstracted from the social and political moment within which the research occurred. This is not to say that the idea that there are Luo rules that ought to be followed does not exist.[2] I argue that the non-negotiable way in which descriptions of 'how things were', thereby echoing a 'glorious past', against references to the risks associated with 'outsiders', is rooted in a national discursive moment that created various permutations of 'us' versus 'them'. By using modals to discuss widow inheritance, gendered language patterns are re-constructed to reflect continuity, historicity and purity as discourses that inform both the construction of the nation and the gendered configurations within it. The positioning of men as authorities due to their arrogation of these linguistic norms centralises homogeneous and hegemonic masculinities. The use of modals and the invocation of metaphors as codes are also grounded in a perceived threat to the nation. The discourse of continuity and purity based on history reconstructs the current threats as a direct result of deviation from the proper course of widow inheritance. Coalescing these discursive energies on the subject becomes a way to consolidate a threatened national position.

Metaphors, silences and subversion

Widow inheritance as a cultural framework and debates generated about it, specifically regarding the 'insider' versus 'outsider' and the protection of boundaries, all act as metaphors to discuss the reconstruction of the Luo nation in the face of larger political contestations. Like modals, the deployment of metaphors in discursive moments was gendered. Metaphors were used to discuss gender and sex and discussions on gender and sex became placeholders for other issues. Discussions on sex and sexualities as they developed around widow inheritance pointed to a robust engagement within a zone that is often layered with 'silences'. There was no overt reference to sex; instead, the metaphor *keto rembi mondo obed mang'ich* was used to reference the need for younger women to control their sexual urges and to avoid being 'hot blooded' by doing the reverse, i.e. 'cooling their blood'.

CAROLINE: Women should not be controlled by their body and should make their blood cold and close that chapter of their lives once they decide. This business of you don't want to be inherited but you are busy spending time in town with men friends is a problem.

GERTRUDE: Inheritance also depends on one's disposition, since some people are mature, but their blood is still hot, so they will want these young boys of 30 years.

The second metaphor is *golo chola*. This is referred to as a rite to cleanse widows. This dirt (*chola*) is removed through sexual intercourse between the widow and the inheritor.

AWINO: What is *chola*?
OGOLLA: '*Chola*' in Luo is something tied around the widow's waist when her husband dies, but after she spends the first night with the inheritor, he would remove it. A woman must have a man, because all rites require that a woman and a man have sexual intercourse, whether it is during planting, harvesting or building a house.

The third metaphor is *yawo ot/golo dala* (opening a house/constructing a house). The idea of 'opening a house' is linked to the importance of a couple officially marking ownership of their home by having sexual intercourse.

TERESA: It [widow inheritance] had an advantage if you had not moved into your own home (*golo dala*), so you might need this man to come and help you construct your own home.

JUDITH: Secondly, when the house gets old and somebody comes to fix it, you will be asked that where is the man in this home so that he can rebuild it, so that's why we got inherited.

The actual construction of a house, or various symbolic acts carried out to signify this (such as the replacement of a corrugated iron sheet or re-thatching a house), are central to the rites related to widow inheritance. The phrase *yawo ot* is a euphemism for sex. While Teresa and Judith refer specifically to the construction of a house, the process of building and moving into a new house has been described as demanding sexual intercourse (see Ogutu, 2001). The construction and eventual *yawo ot* are linked to a discourse on sex, pleasure and choice.

Conclusion

Widow inheritance thus acts as an overarching metaphor for discussions on gendered identities, masculinities and femininities. It is through widow inheritance that space is created for femininities and masculinities to be re-constructed against a romanticised history. This historical context provides the space to reconfigure subversive femininities and reassert power paradigms through taboo and myth as devices within the discourse of 'performing rites'. However, metaphors also articulate 'silences'. Robust conversations occur about sex and sexualities through metaphors. This could easily be missed if the focus were on specific descriptive terms such as sex. These metaphors construct 'respectable' femininities. As a result, the deployment of these metaphors by women renders them respectable, while at the same time allowing them to engage in conversations and alluding to a multiplicity of experiences without destabilising the notion of a 'respectable' widow. It is important to examine the inconsistencies between what is said and how it is said. By simply examining the placement and type of language used, it is possible to miss the opportunities provided by such an approach – primarily the one that creates the fluidity to develop counter-hegemonic narratives. The idea of women as passive actors receiving cultural norms is contradicted by these counternarratives. In adopting Scott's (1987) approach to engaging with language, power and resistance, it is

74 *Gendered language and culture*

possible to see how fluidity, personal narratives and distance from 'authoritative' meta-narratives serve as mechanisms to subvert and redefine a personal relationship to these dominant discourses. Through metaphors, robust conversations around sex and sexuality occur. This demystifies the notion of 'silences' on sexuality amongst this group of women. These metaphors also indicate tensions between non-hegemonic femininities and hegemonic ones, alluding to the renegotiation of individual boundaries and, in turn, redefining the relationship to sexuality. The deployment of metaphors for discussing sex also becomes a tool through which subversive femininities co-exist with hegemonic ones by usurping linguistic practices.

Notes

1 In this chapter I draw on excerpts previously used in other chapters to illustrate how gendered language worked rather than to illustrate how gendered identities were produced which was the focus of the previous chapters.
2 This is discussed in Chapter 2.

6 Conclusion

The primary goal of this book was to examine the gendered discourses conveyed during discussions on widow inheritance, rather than what widow inheritance is or what its merits and demerits may be. In the introduction, 'culture' was recognised as dynamic and therefore prone to change within a context in which different constellations of power exist. It is this cultural discourse of fluidity and change that is deployed to recreate conservative sexualities. Douglas notes:

> When controllers of opinion want a different way of life, taboos lose credibility and the selected view of the universe will be revised. The same impulse to impose order, which brings them into existence, can be supported to be continually modifying or enriching them.
>
> (Douglas, 2002: 5)

The manipulation of 'culture' is evident during moments of 'moral panic' or crises, particularly when community 'boundaries' are challenged. When a community faces an 'external' threat, internal solidarity is fostered (see Burton, 1999; Kandiyoti, 1991; McClintock, 1995; Pape, 1990; Stoler, 2002; Yuval-Davis & Anthias, 1989). This internal solidarity is negotiated and solidified through women's bodies and their sexualities, leading to increased vigilance and surveillance of reproduction, marriage, birth, sex and sexuality. My field research foregrounded knowledge that do not reinscribe homogeneous categories, such as 'Luo widows' or 'African cultural practice'. My analysis of widow inheritance suggests a theoretical approach that moves away from a discourse based on disease, modernity or rights, towards one that can direct engagement with the discursive manipulation of 'culture' and tradition to pursue the goals of those who control power.

Widow inheritance acts as the overall metaphor for pursuing discourses of continuity and purity, through the intricate production of both visible and invisible boundaries that are negotiated around women's bodies. The ritualisation of politics through women's bodies locates local realities within the larger nation/state dynamics. Continuity and purity are sanctioned as central to the pursuit of the nation's goals within the state, with disruption read as a risk to national (Luo) continuity within broader nation/state politics. The modernity/tradition binary, particularly when deployed in collusion with legal state regimes[1] that reify 'culture', becomes a window through which widow inheritance in this case is re-constructed to serve the interests of protagonists on the political stage. Any internal disruption is punished (in this instance) through a complex network of symbols, taboos and rituals. The need to control 'wayward femininities' and sexualities emerges as a response to state oriented struggles around 'Kenyan' national identity. Consequently, the expression of female sexuality in ways that privilege sexual agency, power and choice disrupt normative constructions of femininity. These disruptions are mapped onto communal identities and widow inheritance is used to reset the community's 'boundaries'. The control of women and their sexuality becomes the basis to sustain ideas about community purity, which is evident in the discursive reconstruction of widow inheritance to ascertain fixed boundaries and the need for 'pure' nations. Consequently, any suggested subversion in this zone is powerful. Even though counter-hegemonic narratives by women participants in my research take heteronormativity as given, their narratives nonetheless suggest the destabilising effects of the performance of alternative heterosexuality.

Widow inheritance becomes a useful framework to manage this disruption by defining male power and men's roles through the figure of the *jater* (inheritor). The public/private dichotomy arrogates space to men through a complex network of overt gendered roles, symbols, taboos and linguistic practices. Beyond affirming how fraught this dichotomy is, the field research pointed to how gendered spaces are supported by the creation of roles that cannot be played by women. These roles are primarily associated with decision-making processes in the public (homestead) domain. Consequently, women who challenge gender norms are viewed as 'out of control'. Re-casting sexual agency as 'out of control' emerges as a response from men to a shifting terrain. The control exerted by men, through the figure of *jater*, in terms of activities such as the construction of a house or roles such as 'head of household', is subverted by the instrumentalisation by women of these roles and the power embedded in them. This essentialisation relegates men's power to mere symbolism. The dilemma posed by this essentialisation is articulated by men participants in their construction of women as out of control, where this lack of control manifests in the inability of *joter* to not only ensure that they reproduce, but also that they hand over control of family resources. The production of 'bad' women by men participants emerges as an attempt to reconcile and/or respond to changing masculinities. Poverty and unemployment are deployed to explain changing masculinities. In doing so, these changes are constructed through the prism of state failure and not in response to counter-hegemonic sexualities by women, which 'undermine' male heterosexual power.

In addition, the discursive production of licentious women emerges in connection to women who exercise strategic choices around a *jater*. A woman who has been married before and who is now 'single' presents a different set of power dynamics. They are neither single nor virgins. In instances where children exist, women's authority is already established in the home through motherhood. Widow inheritance rites are designed to manage the liminality created by widowhood and the power instability that comes with it. Yet, it is this liminality that widows use to subvert existing cultural frameworks. The women I interacted with over the course of my research did not present their sexual agency as constrained and repressed; instead, sexual agency was viewed as a powerful negotiating tool. Robust conversations about sexualities point to how 'wayward femininities' and sexualities challenge hegemonic masculinities as sites where patrilineal and patriarchal power is vested. Sexual agency and heterosexual feminine power become political tools with the discursive productions noted throughout this book illustrating how normative gendered order is consistently disrupted. This 'disruption' effectively blurs the public/private dichotomy, re-constructing masculinities and femininities to shift power not only towards women but also within zones defined as masculine. It also places power on the feminine body, which is a contested site and defined as a zone where decisions that affect the community are actively made (around birth, sex, alliances and boundaries).

A key argument throughout this book has been to emphasise the methodological opportunities that exist in examining 'cultural' practices, particularly those that situate normative performances of sexuality, i.e. the construction of hegemonic femininities and masculinities as the basis for re-imagining nations, 'culture' and states. The analytical value of this approach is derived from the evidence of the discursive negotiation, reconstruction and reproduction of sexualities, femininities and masculinities, which defy both fixed gender binaries and nations. The pre-occupation with the 'correct' way to inherit, and the roles of women in the homestead and the re-configuration of widow inheritance, are critical lenses for understanding the shifting political landscapes at both the local and national level. The analysis in this book reveals how sites that are constructed as 'private', 'localised', 'ethnic' and 'feminised' produce robust discourses around communal re-configuration, re-assertion of identity and definition of both internal and external boundaries. In a context where ethnicity is an active mobilisation tool in achieving political goals, these discourses provide useful starting points to understand and deconstruct national tensions. The surveillance of women's bodies and their sexuality is heightened during political moments of crisis, which results in discursive explosions. Attention and analytical weight must therefore be given to embodied, linguistic and discursive practices, for they illuminate the embodied and gendered ritualisation of politics at a local and national level. Approaches that are inattentive to this analytical opportunity do not begin to tackle the aspirations and the spaces that people retreat to, or to 're-write identity'. These spaces are represented by 'cultural practices'. Heteronormativity, gendered identities and subjectivities are forged within these contexts. Sexuality, women's bodies and reproduction as core transmitters of the 'national' (ethnic) project are often abstracted from the mechanisms that reinforce its creation, reproduction and sustenance. Dominant responses within popular discourse in Kenya that continue to place analytical value within structures (the law, parliament, human rights commissions) and the rights framework (through the constitution or national reconciliation processes) as the only way to rewrite Kenya's ethnic political history are limited. While this legal approach may be useful in the interim, it is short-lived.

Bibliography

Adar, K. 1998. 'Ethnicity and ethnic kings: The enduring dual constraint in Kenya's multiethnic democratic electoral experiment.' *Journal of the Third World Spectrum*, 5(2): 71–96.
Adetunji, J. & J. Oni. 1999. 'Rising proportions of young widows and the AIDS epidemic in Africa.' Paper presented at the annual meeting of the American Sociological Association, Chicago, 6–10 August.
Alcoff, L. 1991. 'The problem of speaking for others.' *Cultural Critique*, 20: 5–32.
Amadiume, I. 1997. *Reinventing Africa: Matriarchy, Religion and Culture*. London: Zed Books.
Ambasa-Shisanya, C.R. 2007. 'Widowhood in the era of HIV/AIDS: A case study of Siaya District, Kenya.' *Journal of Social Aspects of HIV/AIDS*, 4(2): 606–15.
Arnfred, S. (ed.). 2004. *Rethinking Sexualities in Africa*. Sweden: Almquist & Wiksell Trycken.
Arutyunova, Angelika & Cindy Clark. 2013. *Watering the leaves, starving the roots: the state of financing for women's rights organizing and gender equality*. Association for Women's Rights in Development (AWID).
Ayikukwei, M., D. Ngare, J.E. Sidle, D. Ayuku, J. Baliddawa & J.Y. Greene. 2007. 'Social and cultural significance of the sexual cleansing ritual and its impact on HIV prevention strategies in western Kenya.' *Sexuality & Culture*, 11(2): 32–50.
Badoe, Y. 2005. 'What makes a woman a witch?' *Feminist Africa*, 5: 37–51.
Bakare-Yusuf, B. 2004. ' "Yoruba's don't do gender": A critical review of Oyeronke Oyewumi's: The Invention of Women: Making an African Sense of Western Gender Discourses.' In CODESRIA. *African Gender Scholarship: Concepts, Methodologies and Paradigms*. Dakar: CODESRIA.
Barnes, T. 2007. 'Politics of the mind and body: Gender and institutional culture in African universities.' *Feminist Africa*, 8: 8–25.
BBC. November 2018. Kenya bans Marie Stopes from offering abortion services. Available at: www.bbc.co.uk/news/world-africa-46254630
Bell, C. 1992. *Ritual Theory, Ritual Practice*. New York: Oxford University Press.
Bennett, J. 2003. Presentation at Curriculum Advisory Group of the Feminist Studies Network, Workshop on Identity, Sex, Gender and Culture. Institute of African Studies Chalets, University of Ghana, Accra, 26–30 May.
———. 2008. 'Editorial: Researching for life: Paradigms and power.' *Feminist Africa*, 11: 1–12.

Bibliography

Bernard, R. 1994. *Research Methods in Anthropology*. London: Sage.

Bloch, M.N. & F. Vavrus. 1998. 'Gender and educational research, policy, and practice in sub-Saharan Africa: Theoretical and empirical problems and prospects.' In J.A. Beoku-Betts, M. Bloch & B.R. Tabachnick (eds.). *Women and Education in Sub-Saharan Africa: Power, Opportunities, and Constraints*. Boulder & London: Lynne Rienner.

Boserup, E. 1970. *Women's Role in Economic Development*. New York: St. Martin's Press.

Boss, Kelly. 2018. 'Six shocking facts about teenage pregnancies in Kenya.' *DailyNation*, 26 November 2018 at 12:39 EAT. Available at: www.standardmedia.co.ke/ureport/story/2001304092/six-shocking-facts-about-teenage-pregnancies-in-kenya

Botwe-Asamoah, K. 2005. *Kwame Nkrumah's Politico-cultural Thought and Policies: An African Centered Paradigm for the Second Phase of the Africa Revolution*. New York & London: Routledge.

Bratton, M. & M. Kimenyi. 2008. 'Voting in Kenya: Putting ethnicity in perspective.' Economics Working Papers series, University of Connecticut, (Online). Available at: http://digitalcommons.uconn.edu/econ wpapers/200809 (Accessed on 28 November 2010).

Bunch, C. 1995. 'Transforming human rights from a feminist perspective.' In J. Peters & A. Wolper (eds.). *Women's Human Rights, Human Rights: International Feminist Perspectives*. London: Routledge.

Burton, A. (ed.). 1999. *Gender, Sexuality and Colonial Modernities*. New York: Routledge.

Butler, J. 1990. *Gender Trouble: Feminism and the Subversion of Identity*. New York: Routledge.

Buvinic, M. 1986. 'Projects for women in the Third World: Explaining their misbehaviour.' *World Development*, 14(5): 653–64.

Caldwell, J., P. Caldwell & P. Quiggin. 1989. 'The social context of AIDS in sub-Saharan Africa.' *Population and Development Review*, 15(2): 185–234.

Cameron, D. (ed.). 1998. *The Feminist Critique of Language: A Reader*. London & New York: Routledge.

———. 2001. *Working with Spoken Discourse*. London: Sage.

Centre for Reproductive Rights (CRR). 2010. *In Harms Way: The Impact of Kenya's Restrictive Abortion Law*. New York: CRR.

Centre for Rights, Education and Awareness (CREAW). 2008. *Wife Inheritance: A Death Sentence Behind the Mask of Culture*. Nairobi: CREAW.

———. 2009. 'Kenyan women call for sex boycott over political deadlock.' 5 May, (Online). Available at: www.portal.creawkenya.org/ . . . /kenyan-women-call-for-sex-boycott-over-political-deadlock-2.pl (Accessed on 28 November 2010).

Chabal, P. 1983. *Amilcar Cabral: Revolutionary Leadership and People's War*. Cambridge: Cambridge University Press.

Chapman, J.R. 1990. 'Violence against women as a violation of human rights.' *Social Justice*, 17(2): 54–70.

Claes, C. 2000. 'The politics of cosmology: An introduction to millenarianism and ethnicity among highland minorities of northern Thailand.' In A. Turton (ed.). *Civility and Savagery: Social Identity in Thai States*. Surrey: Curzon Press.

Cohen, D.W. & E.S. Odhiambo. 1989. *Siaya: The Historical Anthropology of an African Landscape*. Nairobi: Heinemann Kenya.

Cohen, D.W. & E.S. Odhiambo. 1992. *Burying S.M.: The Politics of Knowledge and the Sociology of Power in Africa*. Portsmouth & London: Heinemann & James Currey.

Cornwall, A., S. Correa & S. Jolly. 2008. 'Development with a body: Making the connections between sexuality, human rights and development.' In A. Cornwall, S. Correa & S. Jolly (eds.). *Development with a Body: Sexuality, Human Rights and Development*. London & New York: Zed Books.

Cornwall, A. & S. Jolly. 2009. 'Sexuality and the development industry.' *Development*, 52(1): 5–12.

Correa, S. 2002. 'Sexual rights: Much has been said, much remains to be resolved.' Lecture for the Sexuality, Health and Gender Seminar, Department of Social Sciences, Public Health School, Columbia University, October.

Craviotto, Nerea. 2010. *The Impact of the Global Financial Crisis on Women and Women's Human Rights Across Regions*. Toronto. Association for Women's Rights in Development (AWID).

Daily Nation (Kenya). 2007. 'Elders in the dock over battle against HIV/AIDS in Nyanza.' 17 April.

Denzin, N.K. & Y.S. Lincoln. 1994. *Handbook of Qualitative Research*. London: Sage.

Douglas, M. 2002. *Purity and Danger: An Analysis of the Concepts of Pollution and Taboo*. London: Routledge.

Doyal, L. 1994. 'HIV and AIDS: Putting women on the global agenda.' In L. Doyal, J. Naidoo & T. Wilson (eds.). *AIDS: Setting a Feminist Agenda*. London: Taylor & Francis.

Durkheim, E. 1893. *The Division of Labour in Society*. Transl. George Simpson. Glencoe, IL: Free Press.

Eckert, P. & S. McConnell-Ginet. 2003. *Language and Gender*. Cambridge: Cambridge University Press.

Edelman, M. 1971. *Politics as Symbolic Action*. Chicago: Markham.

Ellen, R.F. (ed.). 1992. *Ethnographic Research: A Guide to General Conduct*. London: Academic Press.

Elshtain, J.B. 1982. 'Feminist discourse and its discontents: Language, power and meaning.' *Signs: Journal of Women in Culture and Society*, 7(3): 603–21.

The English Standard Version Bible: Containing the Old and New Testaments with Apocrypha. 2009. Oxford: Oxford University Press

FEMNET. 2018. 'CSOs Key Recommendations on the Population and Development Agenda in Africa – AADPD+5.' Available at: https://femnet.org/2018/10/csos-key-recommendations-on-the-population-and-development-agenda-in-africa-aadpd5/

Fonow, M. & J. Cook. (eds.). 1991. *Beyond Methodology: Feminist Scholarship as Lived Research*. Bloomington: Indiana University Press.

Foucault, M. 1978. *The History of Sexuality, Vol. 1: An Introduction*. New York: Pantheon Books.

Bibliography

Fraser, N. 1989. *Unruly Practices: Power, Discourse and Gender in Contemporary Social Theory*. Cambridge: Polity Press.

Gellner, E. 1983. *Nations and Nationalism*. Oxford: Basil Blackwell.

Goetz, A.M. 1994. 'From feminist knowledge to data for development: The bureaucratic management of information on women and development.' *IDS Bulletin*, 25(2): 27–36.

Gqola, P. 2001. '*Ufanele uqavile*: Black women, feminisms and postcoloniality in Africa.' *Agenda*, 50: 11–22.

Gwako, M.L. 1998. 'Widow inheritance among the Maragoli of Western Kenya.' *Journal of Anthropological Research*, 54(2): 173–98.

Hammersley, M. & P. Atkinson. 1983. *Ethnography: Principles in Practice*. London: Tavistock.

Hammonds, E.M. 1997. 'Toward a genealogy of black female sexuality: The problematic of silence.' In J. Price & M. Shildrick (eds.). *Feminist Theory and the Body: A Reader*. New York: Routledge.

Harding, S. (ed.). 1987. *Feminism and Methodology*. Bloomington: Open University Press.

Hartsock, N. 1990. 'Foucault on power: A theory for women?' In L. Nicholson (ed.). *Feminism/Postmodernism*. London & New York: Routledge.

Haug, F. 2000. 'Memory work: The key to women's anxiety.' In S. Radstone (ed.). *Memory and Methodology*. Oxford & New York: Berg.

Heald, S. 1995. 'The power of sex: Some reflections on Caldwell's' "African Sexuality" thesis.' *Africa*, 65(4): 489–505.

Helié-Lucas, Marie-Aimée. 1999. 'Women, nationalism, and religion in the Algerian liberation struggle.' In N.C. Gibson (ed.). *Rethinking Fanon: The Continuing Dialogue*. Amherst: Humanity Books.

Hobsbawm, E.J. 1997. *On History*. London: W & N.

Hountondji, P.J. 1976. *African Philosophy: Myth and Reality*. Transl. Henri Evans. Bloomington & Indianapolis: Indiana University Press.

Human Rights Watch (HRW). 2003. *Double Standards: Women's Property Rights Violations in Kenya*, (Online). Available at: www.hrw.org/reports/2003/kenya0303/ (Accessed on 28 November 2010).

Institute of Policy Analysis & Research (IPAR). 2004. 'HIV/AIDS Scourge in Nyanza province: Poverty, culture and behaviour change.' *IPAR Policy Brief*, 10(11), 1–4.

Irigaray, L. 1997. *This Sex Which is not One*. Ithaca: Cornell University Press.

Jackson, S. 2006. 'Gender, sexuality and heterosexuality: The complexity (and limits) of heteronormativity.' *Feminist Theory*, 7(1): 105–21.

Jackson, S. & S. Scott. (eds.). 1996. *Feminism and Sexuality*. New York: Columbia University Press.

Jaggar, A. & S. Bordo. (eds.). 1989. *Gender, Body and Knowledge: Feminist Reconstruction of Being and Knowing*. New Brunswick: Rutgers University Press.

Jaquette, J. 1990. 'Gender and justice in economic development.' In I. Tinker (ed.). *Persistent Inequalities*. Oxford: Oxford University Press.

———. 2006. 'Not so strange bed fellows: Sexuality and international development.' *Development*, 49(1): 77–80.

———. 2007. 'Why the development industry should get over its obsession with bad sex and start to think about pleasure.' IDS Working Paper No. 283. Brighton: IDS.

Kandiyoti, Deniz. 1988. "Bargaining with Patriarchy", *Gender and Society*, Vol. 2, No. 3: 274–290.

Kandiyoti, D. 1991. 'Identity and its discontents: Women and the nation.' *Millennium: Journal of International Studies*, 20(3): 429–43.

Kanyinga, K. & D. Okello. (eds.). 2010. *Tension and Reversals in Democratic Transitions: The Kenyan 2007 General Elections*. Nairobi: IDS & SID.

Kapoor, I. 2004. 'Hyper-self-reflexive development? Spivak on representing the Third World "Other".' *Third World Quarterly*, 25(4): 627–47.

Kenyatta, J. 1977. *Facing Mount Kenya*. London: Heinemann.

Khan, S. 2005. 'Reconfiguring the native informant: Positionality in the global age.' *Signs: Journal of Women in Culture and Society*, 30(4): 2017–35.

Kiaye, G. 1994. 'Aids: Luos facing extinction.' *Daily Nation* (Kenya), 14 October.

Kiragu, J. 1995. 'HIV prevention and women's rights: Working for one means working for both.' *AIDScaptions*, 2(4): 40–6.

Kirwen, M.C. 1979. *African Widows*. Maryknoll: Orbis Books.

Krueger, R.A. 1988. *Focus Groups: A Practical Guide for Applied Research*. London: Sage.

Lakoff, R. 1975. *Language and Women's Place*. Oxford: Oxford University Press.

Lamphere, L., H. Ragone & P. Zavella. (eds.). 1997. *Situated Lives: Gender and Culture in Everyday Life*. New York: Routledge.

Lazreg, M. 1994. *The Eloquence of Silence: Algerian Women in Question*. New York: Routledge.

———. 2002. 'Development: Feminist theory's cul de sac.' In K. Saunders (ed.). *Feminist Post-development Through Rethinking Modernity, Post-colonialism and Representation*. London: Zed Books.

Leach, F. 1998. 'Gender, education and training: An international perspective.' *Gender and Development*, 6(2): 9–18.

Lewis, D. 2003. 'Editorial.' *Feminist Africa*, 2: 1–7.

———. 2004. 'African gender research and post-coloniality: Legacies and challenges.' In CODESRIA (ed.). *African Gender Scholarship: Concepts, Methodologies and Paradigms*. Dakar: CODESRIA.

Longwe, S.H. 2000. 'Towards realistic strategies for women's political empowerment in Africa.' *Gender and Development*, 8(3): 24–30.

Luke, N. 2002. 'Widows and "professional inheritors": Understanding AIDS risk perceptions in Kenya.' Paper presented at the Population Association of America Annual Meetings, Atlanta, 8–11 May.

Lynch, M. 2000. 'Against reflexivity as an academic virtue and source of privileged knowledge.' *Theory, Culture and Society*, 17(3): 26–54.

———. 2006. 'Negotiating ethnicity: Identity politics in contemporary Kenya.' *Review of African Political Economy*, 33(107): 49–65.

MacKinnon, C. 1989. *Toward a Feminist Theory of the State*. Cambridge, MA: Harvard University Press.

Mail & Guardian Online. 2002a. 'Looking a gift blow in the mouth.' 28 June, (Online). Available at: www.mg.co.za (Accessed on 28 November 2010).

———. 2002b. 'Oral sex can save South Africans from Aids.' 14 June, (Online). Available at: www.mg.co.za (Accessed on 28 November 2010).

Malungo, J.R.S. 1999. 'Challenges to sexual behavioural changes in the era of AIDS: Sexual cleansing and levirate marriage in Zambia.' In *Resistances to Behavioural Change to Reduce HIV/AIDS Infection*, (Online). Available at: http://htc.anu.edu.au/pdfs/resistances_ch4.pdf (Accessed on 28 November 2010).

Mama, A. 1996. 'Women and gender studies in the 1990s.' (Online). Available at: www.gwsafrica.org (Accessed on 28 November 2010).

———. 1997. 'Shedding the masks and tearing the veils: Cultural studies for a postcolonial Africa.' In A. Imam, A. Mama & F. Sow (eds.). *Engendering African Social Sciences*. Dakar: CODESRIA.

———. 2001. 'Challenging subjects: Gender and power in African contexts.' In S. Diagne, A. Mama, H. Melber & F. Nyamnjoh (eds.). *Identity and Beyond: Rethinking Africanity*. Discussion Paper No. 12. Uppsala: Nordiska Afrikainstitutet, pp. 9–18.

Mbembe, A. & S. Nuttall. 2004. 'Writing the world from an African metropolis.' *Public Culture*, 16(3): 347–72.

Mbilinyi, M. 1989. '"I'd have been a man": Politics and the labor process in producing personal narratives.' In Personal Narratives Group (eds.). *Interpreting Women's Lives: Feminist Theory and Personal Narratives*. Bloomington: Indiana University Press.

———. 1994. 'Research methodologies in gender issues.' In Ruth Meena (ed.). *Gender in Southern Africa: Conceptual and Theoretical Issues*. Harare: SARIPS.

McClintock, A. 1995. *Imperial Leather: Race, Gender and Sexuality in the Colonial Contest*. New York & London: Routledge.

McFadden, P. 2002. 'Becoming post-colonial: African women changing the meaning of citizenship.' Paper presented at Queens University, Canada, October.

———. 2003. 'Sexual pleasure as feminist choice.' *Feminist Africa*, 2: 50–60.

Mekgwe, P. 2008. 'Theorizing African feminism(s): The "colonial question".' *QUEST: An African Journal of Philosophy/Revue Africaine de Philosophie*, 20: 11–22.

Merton, R.K., M. Fiske & P.L. Kendall. 1990. *The Focused Interview: A Manual of Problems and Procedures*, 2nd ed. London: Collier Macmillan.

Mikell, G. 1997. *African Feminism: The Politics of Survival in Sub-Saharan Africa*. Philadelphia: University of Pennsylvania Press.

Miller, C. & K. Swift. 1976. *Words and Women*. New York: Doubleday.

Miriam, K. 2007. 'Toward a phenomenology of sex-right: Reviving radical feminist theory of compulsory sexuality.' *Hypatia*, 22(1): 210–28.

Mohanty, T.C. 2002. '*Under Western Eyes* revisted: Feminist solidarity through anticapitalist struggles.' *Signs: Journal of Women in Culture and Society*, 28(2): 499–534.

Morton, S. 2003. *Gayatri Chakravorty Spivak*. London: Routledge.
Moser, C. 1993. *Gender Planning and Development: Theory, Practice and Training*. London: Routledge.
Mudimbe, V.Y. 1988. *The Invention of Africa: Gnosis, Philosophy and the Order of Language*. London. James Currey.
Mupotsa, D. & L. Mhishi. 2008. 'This little rage of poetry: Researching gender and sexuality.' *Feminist Africa*, 11: 97–107.
Mutunga, K. 2010. 'Stop the tribal tagging, we are simply Kenyan.' *Daily Nation* (Kenya), 6 September.
Mwenda, K. 2007. 'African customary law and customs: Changes in the culture of sexual cleansing of widows and the marrying of a deceased brother's widow.' *Gonzaga Journal of International Law*, 11(1), (Online). Available at: www.gonzagajil.org/pdf/volume11/ (Accessed on 24 November 2010).
Narayan, U. 1989. 'The project of feminist epistemology: Perspectives of a north western feminist.' In A. Jaggar & S. Bordo (eds.). *Gender, Body and Knowledge: Feminist Reconstruction of Being and Knowing*. Rutgers: Rutgers University Press.
National AIDS Control Council (NACC). 2000. *Kenya National HIV/AIDS Strategic Plan, 2000–2005*. Nairobi: Office of the President & NACC.
National AIDS/STD Control Programme & Ministry of Health (NASCOP & MOH). 1998. *Report of the Second National HIV/AIDS/STD Conference: Lessons Learned*. Nairobi: NASCOP & MOH.
Ndisi, J.W. 1974. *A Study in the Economic and Social Life of the Luo of Kenya*. Lund: Berlingska Boktryckeriet.
Nessman, R. 1999. 'Out of Africa comes change but not without controversy.' *Associated Press*, 6 April.
New York Times. 2004. 'Opinion: Africa's homeless widows.' 16 June, (Online). Available at: www.nytimes.com/2004/06/16/opinion/16WED1.html?th (Accessed on 24 November 2010).
Nkrumah, K. 1961. *I Speak of Freedom: A Statement of African Ideology*. London: Heinemann.
Ntozi, James P.M. 1997. 'Widowhood, remarriage and migration during the HIV/AIDS epidemic in Uganda.' *Health Transition Review*, Supplement to Volume 7: 125–44.
Nyanzi, S., Justine Nassimbwa, Vincent Kayizzi & Strivan Kabanda et al. 2005. '"African sex is dangerous!" Renegotiating "ritual sex" in contemporary Masaka district.' Draft document.
Nyerere, J. 1967. 'Tanzania Policy on Foreign Affairs.' Address at the TANU National Conference, Mwanza, 16 October.
Nyerere, J. 1968. *Ujamaa: Essays on Socialism*. Dar es Salaam: Oxford University Press.
Obbo, C. 1986. 'Some East African widows.' In Betty Potash (ed.). *Widows in African Societies*. Stanford: Stanford University Press.
Ocholla-Ayayo, A.B.C. 1980. *The Luo Culture: A Reconstruction of the Material Culture Patterns of a Traditional African Society*. Wiesbaden: Franz Steiner.

Bibliography

———. 1996. *Psychical, Social and Cultural Issues Relating to HIV/AIDS Containment and Transmission in Africa with Special Reference to Kenya.* Nairobi: Population Studies Research Institute & UON.

Odinga-Odinga, J. 1967. *Not Yet Uhuru.* London: Heinemann.

Ogot, B. 1967. *History of the Southern Luo: Migration and Settlement.* Nairobi: East African Publishing House.

Ogutu, G.E.M. 1995. *Ker Jaramogi Is Dead: Who Shall Lead My People? Reflections on Past, Present and Future Luo Thought and Practice.* Kisumu: Palwa Research.

———. 2001. *Ruth: Change and Continuity in Luo Widowhood Rights and Privileges: Leviratic Union (Wife/Husband 'Inheritance') Revisited.* Kisumu: Sundowner Institute Press.

Ojwang, J.B. & J.N.K. Mugambi. (eds.). 1989. *The S.M. Otieno Case: Death and Burial in Modern Kenya.* Nairobi: Nairobi University Press.

Okech, A. 2013. 'Where Kenyan women stand: Assault on Hon. Rachel Shebesh.' Available at: https://femnet.org/2013/09/where-kenyan-women-stand-assault-on-hon-rachel-shebesh/

Okoth, D. 2006. 'Luanda Magere: A legend whose spirit lives on.' (Online). Available at: www.afroarticles.com/article . . . /Luanda-Magere – A. . . /4582 (Accessed on 24 November 2010).

Omboki, A. 2018. 'Unsafe abortions kill seven Kenyans daily.' *Daily Nation*, 21 September 2018. Available at: www.nation.co.ke/news/Unsafe-abortions-kill-seven-Kenyans-daily/1056-4769952-i6kd8pz/index.html

Ong, A. 1997. 'Spirits of resistance.' In L. Lamphere, H. Ragone & P. Zavella (eds.). *Situated Lives: Gender and Culture in Everyday Life.* New York: Routledge.

Onyango-Obbo, C. 2004. 'Tale of the naked Luo widow.' *Daily Nation* (Kenya), 22 January.

Oriang, L. 2004. 'Tradition or not, I'll have none of it.' *Daily Nation* (Kenya), 18 June.

Owen, M. 1996. *A World of Widows.* London: Zed Books.

Oxfam International. 2008. *From Poverty to Power: How Active Citizens and Effective States Can Change the World.* London: Oxfam International.

Oyewumi, O. 1997. *The Invention of Women: Making an African Sense of Western Gender Discourse.* Minneapolis: University of Minnesota Press.

———. 2002. 'Conceptualising gender: The Eurocentric foundations of feminist concepts and the challenge of African epistemologies.' *Jenda: A Journal of Culture and African Women Studies*, 2(1), (Online). Available at: www.africaresource.com/jenda/vol2.1/oyewumi.html (Accessed on 24 November 2010).

Oyugi, W. 1994. 'Uneasy alliance: Party-state relations in Kenya.' In W. Oyugi (ed.). *Politics and Administration in East Africa.* Nairobi: East African Publishers.

———. 2002. 'Politicized ethnic conflict in Kenya: A periodic phenomenon.' In B. Abdalla & A. Said (eds.). *Breaking Barriers, Creating New Hopes: Democracy, Civil Society and Good Governance in Africa.* Oxford: African Books Collective.

Packer, C.A.A. 2002. *Using Human Rights to Change Tradition: Traditional Practices Harmful to Women's Reproductive Health in Sub-Saharan Africa.* Utrecht: Intersentia.

Pala, O.A. 1980. 'Daughters of the lake and rivers: Colonisation and land rights of Luo women in Kenya.' In M. Etienne & E. Leacock (eds.). *Women and Colonisation: Anthropological Perspectives*. New York: Praeger.

Pape, J. 1990. 'Black and white: The perils of sex in colonial Zimbabwe.' *Journal of Southern African Studies*, 16(4): 699–710.

Pereira, C. 2003. 'Where angels fear to tread? Some thoughts on Patricia McFadden's "Sexual pleasure as feminist choice".' *Feminist Africa*, 2: 61–5.

———. 2005. 'Zina and transgressive heterosexuality in northern Nigeria.' *Feminist Africa*, 5: 52–79.

———. 2009. 'Interrogating norms: Feminists theorizing sexuality, gender and heterosexuality.' *Development*, 52(1): 18–24, (Online). Available at: www.sidint.org/development (Accessed on 24 November 2010).

Personal Narratives Group (PNG). 1989. *Interpreting Women's Lives: Feminist Theory and Personal Narratives*. Bloomington: Indiana University Press.

Petchesky, R. 2000. 'Links between reproductive and sexual rights and social development: Charting the course of transnational women's NGOs.' United Nations Research Institute for Social Development, Occasional Paper No. 8. New York: UNRISD.

Potash, B. 1978. 'Some aspects of marital stability in a rural Luo community.' *Africa*, 48: 380–97.

———. 1986. 'Wives of the graves: Widows in a rural Luo community.' In B. Potash (ed.). *Widows in African Societies: Choices and Constraints*. Stanford: Stanford University Press.

Presser, L. 2005. 'Negotiating power and narrative in research: Implications for feminist methodology.' *Signs: Journal of Women in Culture and Society*, 3(4): 2067–90.

Prince, R. 2007. 'Salvation and traditions: Configurations of faith in a time of death.' *Journal of Religion in Africa*, 37: 84–115.

Ratele, K. 2006. 'Ruling masculinity and sexuality.' *Feminist Africa*, 6: 48–64.

Razavi, S. & C. Miller. 1995. 'From WID to GAD: Conceptual shifts in the women and development discourse.' Occasional Paper No. 1. Geneva: United Nations Research Institute for Social Development.

Republic of Kenya. 2008. Office of the Prime Minister & Ministry of State for Planning. n.d. *Kisumu East District Development Plan 2008–2012*. Nairobi: Government Printer.

Rubin, G. 1975. 'The traffic in women: Notes on the "political economy" of sex.' In Rayna R. Reiter (ed.). *Toward an Anthropology of Women*. New York: Monthly Review Press.

———. 1984. 'Thinking sex: Notes for a radical theory of the politics of sexuality.' In V. Carole (ed.). *Pleasure and Danger: Exploring Female Sexuality*. Boston: Routledge.

Saunders, K. (ed.). 2002. *Feminist Post-development Through Rethinking Modernity, Post-colonialism and Representation*. London: Zed Books.

Sengendo, J. & E.K. Sekatawa. 1999. 'A cultural approach to HIV/AIDS prevention and care: Uganda's experience.' UNESCO/UNAIDS Research Project, Cultural

Bibliography

Policies for Development Unit. Studies and Reports, Special Series, No. 1, (Online). Available at: www.unesco.org (Accessed on 24 November 2010).

Scott, C.V. 1995. *Gender and Development: Rethinking Modernization and Dependency Theory*. Boulder: Lynne Rienner.

Scott, J. 1987. *Domination and the Arts of Resistance: Hidden Transcripts*. New Haven: Yale University Press.

Sharpe, J. & G. Spivak. 2002. 'A conversation with Gayatri Chakravorty Spivak: Politics and the imagination.' *Signs: Journal of Women in Culture and Society*, 28(2): 609–24.

Sleap, B. 2001. 'Widows and AIDS: Redefinitions and challenges.' Panos AIDS Programme Widows Without Rights, 7 February, (Online). Available at: www.widowsrights.org/Widows%20and%20AIDS.pdf (Accessed on 24 November 2010).

Smith, H.F. 1997. Ring Ding in a Tight Corner in Alexander, J. & Mohanty, C. (eds). 1997. Feminist Genealogies, Colonial Legacies, Democratic Futures: New York. Routledge.

Spender, D. 1980. *Man-made Language*. London: Routledge & Kegan Paul.

Spivak, G. 1988. 'Can the subaltern speak?' In C. Nelson & L. Grossberg (eds.). *Marxism and Interpretation of Culture*. Chicago: University of Illinois Press.

———. 1993. *Outside in the Teaching Machine*. New York: Routledge.

Stamp, P. 1991. 'Burying Otieno: The politics of gender and ethnicity.' *Signs: Journal of Women in Culture and Society*, 16(4): 808–45.

Star Reporter. 2018. 'Varsity student abducted with Nation journalist found dead in Kodera forest.' *The Star*, 5 September 2018. Available at: www.the-star.co.ke/news/2018/09/05/varsity-student-abducted-with-nation-journalist-found-dead-in-kodera_c1813722

Steady, F.C. 1981. *The Black Woman Cross-culturally*. Cambridge, MA: Schenkman.

———. 2002. 'An investigative framework for gender research in Africa in the new millennium.' Paper presented at the conference on African Gender Research in the New Millennium: Perspectives, Directions and Challenge, CODESRIA, Cairo, 8–10 April.

Stoler, A. 2002. *Carnal Knowledge and Imperial Power: Race and the Intimate in Colonial Rule*. Los Angeles: University of California Press.

Stromquist, N.P. 1999. 'Women's education in the twenty-first century: Balance and prospects.' In R.F. Arnove & C.A. Torres (eds.). *Comparative Education: The Dialectic of the Global and the Local*. Lanham: Rowman & Littlefield.

Sweetman, C. 2008. 'How title deeds make sex safer: Women's property rights in an era of HIV.' In Oxfam International (ed.). *From Poverty to Power: How Active Citizens and Effective States Can Change the World*. London: Oxfam International.

Tamale, S. 2003. 'Out of the closet: Unveiling sexuality discourses in Uganda.' *Feminist Africa*, 2: 42–9.

———. 2005. 'Eroticism, sexuality and women's secrets among the Baganda: A critical analysis.' *Feminist Africa*, 5: 9–36.

———. 2008. 'The right to culture and the culture of rights: A critical perspective on women's sexual rights in Africa.' *Feminist Legal Studies*, 16: 47–69.

Bibliography 89

Teng'o, D. 2003. 'An old Luo myth is retold with a modern touch.' 6 December, (Online). Available at: http://allafrica.com/stories/200312060093.html (Accessed on 24 November 2010).

Thomas, L. 1997. '"*Ngaitana*" (I will circumcise myself)": The gender and generational politics of the 1956 ban on clitoridectomy in Meru, Kenya.' In N.R. Hunt, T. Liu & J. Quataert (eds.). *Gendered Colonialisms in African History*. Oxford & Malden, MA: Blackwell.

———. 2005. *Politics of the Womb: Women, Reproduction and the State in Kenya*. Kampala: Fountain.

Thongori, J. 2009. 'Gender responsive legislative reform: An assessment of the Marriage Bill 2007.' Paper presented at the Heinrich Böll Foundation's Gender Forum, Nairobi, 30 April.

Thorne, B., C. Kramarae & N. Henley. (eds.). 1983. *Language, Gender and Society*. Rowley: Newbury House.

Tinker, I. (ed.). 1990. *Persistent Inequalities*. Oxford: Oxford University Press.

Tuhiwai-Smith, L. 2006. *Decolonising Methodologies*. London: Zed Books.

Turner, V. 1969. *The Ritual Process: Structure and Anti-structure*. Chicago: Aldine.

Visweswaran, K. 1994. *Fictions of Feminist Ethnography*. Minneapolis: University of Minnesota Press.

Wahome, A.M. 2001. 'Gender equality under customary law.' Paper presented at an annual workshop on the Role of Civil and Customary Law in Relation to Women Property Rights, Namibia, 5–8 March.

White, L. 2001. 'True stories: Narrative event, history and blood in the Lake Victoria basin.' In L. White, S.F. Miescher & D.W Cohen (eds.). *African Words, African Voices: Critical Practices in Oral History*. Bloomington: Indiana University Press.

Wilson, K. 2011. '"Race", gender and neoliberalism: Changing visual representations in development.' *Third World Quarterly*, 32(2): 315–31.

Wilson-Tagoe, N. 2003. 'Representing culture and identity: African women writers and national cultures.' *Feminist Africa*, 2: 25–41.

Win, E.J. 2004, 'Not very poor, powerless or pregnant: The African woman forgotten by development.' *IDS Bulletin*, 35(4): 61–5.

Wortel, E. 2004. 'Isn't it time to change the inheritance law?' *The Guardian*, 5 July.

Yuval-Davis, N. 1997. *Gender and Nation*. London: Sage.

Yuval-Davis, N. & F. Anthias. (eds.). 1989. *Woman-Nation-State*. London: Macmillan.

Index

abortion 17
Adetunji, J. 31
African culture 6; gender and 11–12
African feminist scholarship 1–2; book structure and 6–9; memory and truth in 5–6; methodology in 2–4; research methods 4–5
African liberation movements 11
Ambasa-Shisanya, C.R. 30
AWID 14
Ayikukuwei, M. 25, 27, 39, 40

bargaining theory model 32, 36, 38–9
Bell, C. 26
body politics and sexuality 15–16, 27–8, 78
borders, defining 57–8
Boserup, E. 13
bought relation 40n5
boundaries *see* discursive boundaries
Bunge la Wananchi 17
Burton, A. 11

chike 33
chira 25, 28, 48–9
Christian traditions 32–3
cleansing rituals 24–5, 27, 49
Correa, S. 36
counter-narratives 57
cultural prescriptions 31

discursive boundaries: defining borders and constructing 57–8; 'insider' 58–9; 'outsider' 59–64; political expediency in 63–4; purity discourse in 60–1, 63, 75–6; widow inheritance as vehicle for defining 64
disembodied and disciplining ritual practices 26–8
Douglas, M. 28, 40, 59, 75
Durkheim, E. 26

economic development and women 14
Edelman, M. 26
empowerment 31–2, 34, 36, 37–8, 40n8

Facing Mount Kenya 6
focus group discussions (FGDs) 3–5

gender: African culture and 11–12; discourses around sexuality and 55–6; economic development and 14; politics of 42–9; post flag independence 12–15; social construction of 34; wayward femininities and 49–53; widow inheritance and norms of 23–5, 41–2
gendered linguistic practices 67–72
Goetz, A.M. 13
golo chola 28, 72
Gwako, M.L. 31

heterosexual marital bonds 21–3
hidden transcripts 66–7
HIV/AIDS pandemic 27, 28–32, 39, 48–9; religion as trope in 32–3, 39–40

Institute of Policy Analysis and Research (IPAR) 30
Jackson, S. 40
Jamwa 59–64
JusticeforSharon 18

Kandiyoti, D. 13
Kenya: debates on sexuality in 17–19; national culture of 6; political activism by women of 17–19; post-colonial government in 6, 16; Women in Development (WID) framework in 12–13; women's rights in 34–7
Kenyatta, J. 6
Kidero, E. 17
KideroMustGo 18
kusalazya 31

Lakoff, R. 66
language 66–7; gendered linguistic practices in 67–72; hidden transcripts in 66–7; metaphors, silences, and subversion in 72–3; widow inheritance as overarching metaphor and 73
Lawal, A. 15, 18n1
levirates *(joter)* 3
Lewis, D. 6, 12
Luanda Magere, story of 61, 65n3
Luo community 20–1; autonomy of widows in 24; Christian religion and 32–3; disembodied and disciplining ritual practices in 26–8; heterosexual marital bonds in 21–3; 'insiders' in 58–9; 'outsider' in 59–64; patriarchal society of 23, 37; respectable femininities in 49, 53–5; ritual cleansing in 25, 27; women's rights in 34–7

male power 45–6, 76–7
Malungo, J.R.S. 25, 31
marriage, norms of heterosexual 21–3, 35, 78; religion and 32–3, 39–40, 40n6–7
McFadden, P. 1, 16–17
metaphors 72–3

Mhishi, L. 16
Miller, C. 66
modern/tradition binary 36–7, 38
Mohanty, T.C. 12
moral panic 75
Mupotsa, D. 16

National AIDS Control Council (NACC) 30
national culture 6, 75, 76; HIV/AIDS pandemic and 30; widow inheritance in 20–1
neoliberalism 14
Not Yet Uhuru 6
Nyanzi, S. 24, 30
Nyerere, J. 6, 11

Oginga-Odinga, J. 6
Ogutu, G. 22–5, 27, 32, 39, 40n4
Oni, J. 31
Otieno, S. 18, 36–7, 62
Otieno, W. 56n4

patriarchal society 23, 37
People's parliament 19n3
Pereira, C. 15–16
personhood 27
political expediency 63–4
politics: body 15–16, 27–8, 78; of gender 42–9; political expediency in 63–4
post-colonial Africa 6, 11–12, 16
Potash, B. 24
power: male 45–6, 76–7; of widows upon their husband's death 46–8; of women in the private/public domain 44–5, 51, 76–7
pregnancy 17–18; in widows 24
Prince, R. 33
public/private roles of women 41, 43–4, 76–7
purity discourse 60–1, 63, 75–6

Ratele, K. 16
Razavi, S. 13
reconstruction of culture 30
religion 32–3, 39–40, 40n6–7
reproduction and respectable femininities 53–5

respectable femininities 49, 53–5
ritual cleansing 3, 24–5, 27, 49

Scott, C.V. 66–7, 73–4
Scott, S. 40
Senghor, S. 6
sexuality: African feminist scholarship on 1–2; body politics and 15–16, 27–8, 78; debates on, in Kenya 17–19; discourses around gender and 55–6; HIV/AIDS pandemic and 27, 28–32, 32–3, 39–40, 48–9; purity discourse and 60–1, 63; 'safer' zones of 16
Shebesh, R. 18
silences 72–3
Sleap, B. 29
S.M. Otieno vs Wambui Otieno 36–7, 56n4, 62, 65n4
Spender, D. 66
Spivak, G. 7
Stoler, A. 11
subversion, linguistic 72–3
Sweetman, C. 36
Swift, K. 66

Thomas, L. 12, 16
Thorne, B. 66
Turner, V. 26

Ujamaa 6, 11

Wahome, A.M. 34
Warembo ni Yes campaign 17
widow inheritance: bargaining theory of 32, 36, 38–9; commonalities in scholarship on 37–40; as cultural practice 20–1; disembodied and disciplining ritual practices with 26–8; empowerment and 31–2, 34, 36, 37–8, 40n8; explanatory accounts of 7–8; gender norms and 23–5, 41–2; heterosexual marital bonds and 21–3; inheritors appointed in 24, 27; 'insider' and 58–9; language and (*see* language); as metaphor and tool for re-assertion of sexual boundaries 9; metaphors, silences, and subversion in 72–3; modernity/tradition binary and 36–7, 38; 'outsider' and 59–64; as overall metaphor for discourses of continuity and purity 75–6; power of women and 46–8, 76–7; religion as trope in 32–3, 39–40, 40n6–7; ritual cleansing and 24–5, 27, 49; sexualisation of widows and 55; terminology 20; wayward femininities in 49–53; women's rights and 34–7; younger men constructed as victims and 52; *see also* women
women: body politics of 15–16, 27–8; economic development for 14; empowerment of 31–2, 34, 36, 37–8, 40n8; gendered linguistic practices and 67–72; HIV/AIDS in 27, 28–32, 39–40, 48–9; political activism by 17–19; power of, in the private/public domain 43–4, 51, 76–7; public roles of 44; respectable femininities and 49, 53–5; ritual cleansing of 24–5, 27, 49; sexualisation of widowed 55; wayward femininities in 49–53; widow inheritance and rights of 34–7; younger men constructed as victims of 52; *see also* widow inheritance
Women in Development (WID) framework 12–13
Women's Role in Economic Development 13

yawo ot 72–3

zina 15